BIBLE CONTRADICTIONS AND THEIR RESOLUTIONS
Answering Purported Biblical Self-Contradictions

BIBLE CONTRADICTIONS AND THEIR RESOLUTIONS

Answering Purported Biblical
Self-Contradictions

John Teller

LOGOS LIGHT

BIBLE CONTRADICTIONS AND THEIR RESOLUTIONS
Answering Purported Biblical Self-Contradictions

ISBN (13) (Paperback): 978-1-68109-094-8
ISBN (10) (Paperback): 1-68109-094-5
ISBN (13) (ePub): 978-1-68109-095-5
ISBN (10) (ePub): 1-68109-095-3

LOGOS LIGHT

LogosLight™
an imprint of TellerBooks™
TellerBooks.com/LogosLight

t TellerBooks

www.TellerBooks.com

Manufactured in the U.S.A.

Cover: © Jeff Jacobs 1990 (Pixabay Creative Commons License)

NOTE: Unless otherwise stated herein, all biblical Scriptures quoted herein are taken from the New King James Version or New International Version translations.

DISCLAIMER: The opinions, views, positions and conclusions expressed in this volume reflect those of the individual author and not necessarily those of the publisher or any of its imprints, editors or employees.

ABOUT THE IMPRINT

The LogosLight™ imprint first started with the collection The Church Fathers Speak, a compilation of the voices of the early Church fathers and their teachings on sanctity and Christ-like living. This ancient wisdom guides the reader on the path to cultivating holiness that yields self-dominion, patience, and virtue.

LogosLight™ has since grown to encompass Christian poetry and inspirational books, translations of the Bible and Hebrew Scriptures, and various Christian records and Liturgies.

LogosLight™ books also examine the role of Judeo-Christian thought on the formation of Western civic institutions, the moral foundations of just societies, and the role of faith in civil governance.

LOGOS LIGHT

CONTENTS

Contents 15

ABBREVIATIONS

English Translations of the Bible:

ASV .... American Standard Version
BBE .... Bible in Basic English
Darby .... Darby Bible
ESV .... English Standard Version
ISV .... International Standard Version
KJV .... King James Version
MKJV .... Modern King James Version
NIV .... New International Version
NKJV .... New King James Version
RSV .... Revised Standard Version

Books of the Bible:

1Ch .... 1 Chronicles
1Co .... 1 Corinthians
1Jn .... 1 John
1Ki .... 1 Kings
1Pe .... 1 Peter
1Sa .... 1 Samuel
1Th .... 1 Thessalonians
1Ti .... 1 Timothy
2Ch .... 2 Chronicles
2Co .... 2 Corinthians
2Jn .... 2 John
2Ki .... 2 Kings
2Pe .... 2 Peter
2Sa .... 2 Samuel
2Th .... 2 Thessalonians
2Ti .... 2 Timothy
3Jo .... 3 John
Acts .... Book of Acts
Amos .... Book of Amos
Col .... Colossians
Dan .... Daniel

Deu ....Deuteronomy
Ecc.................Ecclesiastes
Eph ....Ephesians
Est ....Esther
Exo ....Exodus
Eze.................Ezekiel
Ezr ....Book of Ezra
Gal.................Galatians
Gen ....Genesis
Hab ....Habakkuk
Hag ....Haggai
Heb ....Hebrews
Hos ....Hosea
Isa ....Isaiah
Jas ....James
Jer ....Jeremiah
Job ....Book of Job
Joel ....Book of Joel
John ....Gospel of John
Jon ....Jonah
Jos ....Joshua
Jude ....Book of Jude
Jdg ....Judges
Lam ....Lamentations
Lev ....Leviticus
Luke ....Gospel of Luke
Mal ....Malachi
Mark ....Gospel of Mark
Mat ....Gospel of Matthew
Mic ....Micah
Nah.................Nahum
Neh ....Nehemiah
Num.................Numbers
Oba ....Obadiah
Phm ....Philemon
Php ....Philippians
Pro ....Proverbs
Psa ....Psalms
Rev ....Revelation

Rom .... Romans
Ruth .... Book of Ruth
Son .... Song of Solomon
Tit .... Titus
Zec .... Zechariah
Zep .... Zephaniah

CHAPTER 1. INTRODUCTION

Skeptics, atheists and agnostics have long argued that the Bible is riddled with self-contradictions that render it unreliable. They point to many purported contradictions that undermine the Bible's claim to being the Word of God. Who carried Jesus' cross: Simon, as reported in the Gospel of Luke, or Jesus, as reported in the Gospel of John? Did a centurion plead with Jesus to heal his servant, as Matthew reports, or did he send elders of the Jews to plead with Jesus, as Luke reports? Did 40,000 horsemen die in battle with David, as 2 Samuel reports, or did 40,000 foot soldiers die, as 1 Chronicles reports? Did both thieves mock Jesus on the cross, as narrated by the Gospel of Matthew, or did only one thief mock him, as narrated by the Gospel of Mark?

Many students of the Bible, upon reading these passages, throw their hands up in frustration and conclude that the Bible cannot be divinely inspired. Some Christians, unable to explain these difficulties, walk away from the faith. Others, when pressed, concede that they do not have explanations but believe reasonable explanations exist, though they cannot articulate any. Muslims and Mormons use the apparent contradictions of the Bible to support their claims that the Bible, in its current form, is a corruption of the original message of God.

Now there is a response to these claims. This book defends the divine inspiration of the Bible and demonstrates with clarity that the so-called "contradictions" of the Bible are not contradictions at all. A careful study of the Scriptures in their original context and in light of the nuances in which they were originally written vindicates the Bible from claims of errancy.

This book examines the "contradictions" most frequently cited by the detractors of Christianity and offers reasoned explanations. Armed with this book, Christians can respond to their critics and rest assured that their faith is not incompatible with logic. There are, in fact, reasonable responses to the claims made by Christianity's detractors and logical arguments in support of the Bible's inerrancy.

CHAPTER 2. ACCOUNTS OF THE CENTURION WHOSE SERVANT WAS HEALED (MAT 8, LUKE 7)

I. OVERVIEW

In Mathew 8, the centurion personally came before Jesus, but in Luke 7, he sent elders to Jesus and then a second delegation of friends to speak with Jesus.

	Matthew 8	Luke 7
A centurion pleads with Jesus to heal his paralyzed servant. Jesus agrees to heal him.	Mat 8:5 Now when Jesus had entered Capernaum, a centurion came to Him, pleading with Him, Mat 8:6 saying, "Lord, my servant is lying at home paralyzed, dreadfully tormented." Mat 8:7 And Jesus said to him, "I will come and heal him."	
A centurion sent elders of the Jews to plead with Jesus to heal the		Luke 7:2 And a certain centurion's servant, who was dear to him, was sick and ready to die. Luke 7:3 So when he

centurion's servant. The Jews plead with Jesus.		heard about Jesus, he sent elders of the Jews to Him, pleading with Him to come and heal his servant. Luke 7:4 And when they came to Jesus, they begged Him earnestly, saying that the one for whom He should do this was deserving, Luke 7:5 "for he loves our nation, and has built us a synagogue."
The centurion said (Mat) / the centurion sent friends to Jesus say (Luke) that the centurion was not worthy for Jesus to enter his house.	Mat 8:8 The centurion answered and said, "*Lord, I am not worthy that You should come under my roof. But only speak a word, and my servant will be healed.* Mat 8:9 *For I also am a man under authority, having soldiers under me. And I say to this one, 'Go,' and he goes; and to another, 'Come,' and he comes; and to my servant, 'Do this,' and he does it.*"	Luke 7:6 Then Jesus went with them. And when He was already not far from the house, the centurion sent friends to Him, saying to Him, "Lord, do not trouble Yourself, for *I am not worthy that You should enter under my roof*. Luke 7:7 Therefore I did not even think myself worthy to come to You. *But say the word, and my servant will be healed.* Luke 7:8 *For I also am a man placed under authority,*

		having soldiers under me. And I say to one, 'Go,' and he goes; and to another, 'Come,' and he comes; and to my servant, 'Do this,' and he does it."
Jesus marveled at the centurion's faith	Mat 8:10 *When Jesus heard it, He marveled, and said to those who followed, "Assuredly, I say to you, I have not found such great faith, not even in Israel!*	Luke 7:9 *When Jesus heard these things, He marveled at him, and turned around and said to the crowd that followed Him, "I say to you, I have not found such great faith, not even in Israel!"*
Many will come from the east and the west to the kingdom, but the sons will be cast out.	Mat 8:11 And I say to you that many will come from east and west, and sit down with Abraham, Isaac, and Jacob in the kingdom of heaven. Mat 8:12 But the sons of the kingdom will be cast out into outer darkness. There will be weeping and gnashing of teeth."	
Jesus assured the centurion that the servant	Mat 8:13 Then Jesus said to the centurion, "Go your way; and as you have believed, so let it be done for you."	

would be healed.		
The servant was healed remotely.	And *his servant was healed* that same hour.	Luke 7:10 And those who were sent, returning to the house, found *the servant well who had been sick*.

II. PROPOSED EXPLANATION

1. When an Agent Speaks on Behalf of a Principal, the Words Are Imputed to the Principal

The accounts in Matthew and Luke are not necessarily contradictions. When a person undertakes an act or states certain words within his capacity as an agent of a third party, the acts and words of the agent can be attributed and imputed to the third party as though the third party undertook the acts or spoke the words himself. Therefore, if A grants B a power of attorney to sell his home and B goes about selling A's home, it can be said that A sold his home, even though it was B that actually marketed the home, accepted an offer and signed the closing documents on A's behalf.

We see the attribution of acts to third parties throughout the Bible. For example, when John wrote, "Pilate took Jesus and scourged Him" (John 19:1), he meant that Pilate ordered it to be done, not that he did it himself. It would be highly out of the ordinary for a governor to personally administer the corporal punishment of a prisoner.

2. The Fact that the Centurion Spoke through Agents Is a Detail Omitted in Matthew

Most likely, the centurion was speaking through a delegation of Jewish elders and friends. The words spoken by the delegation in Luke 7:6 to 7:8 are virtually identical to those attributed to the centurion in Matthew 8:8 and 8:9. Most likely, the extra detail with respect to the means through which the centurion spoke with Jesus was omitted from Matthew, but included in Luke, who was arguably the most thorough of the Evangelists. Luke undertook thorough research when compiling his Gospel, which opens with:

> Luke 1:1 Inasmuch as many have taken in hand to set in order a narrative of those things which have been fulfilled among us,
> Luke 1:2 just as those who from the beginning were eyewitnesses and ministers of the word delivered them to us,
> Luke 1:3 it seemed good to me also, having had perfect understanding of all things from the very first, to write to you an orderly account, most excellent Theophilus,
> Luke 1:4 that you may know the certainty of those things in which you were instructed.

It thus appears that Luke was being more specific than Matthew and Matthew was using a common form of speech whereby an agent's words are attributed to the principal. The two accounts can thus be viewed as harmonious.

CHAPTER 3. ARE ALL OF OUR PRAYER PETITIONS ANSWERED?

I. OVERVIEW

1. Scriptures that Show All Prayers Are Granted

The following Scriptures imply that whatever we ask will be given to us:

- Mat 7:7 Ask, and it will be given to you; seek, and you will find; knock, and it will be opened to you. Mat 7:8 For everyone who asks receives, and he who seeks finds, and to him who knocks it will be opened.
- Mat 18:19 Again I say to you that if two of you agree on earth concerning anything that they ask, it will be done for them by My Father in heaven.
- Luke 11:9 And I say to you, Ask and it shall be given you. Seek and you shall find. Knock and it shall be opened to you. Luke 11:10 For everyone who asks receives. And he who seeks finds. And to him who knocks it shall be opened.

2. Empirical Evidence and Biblical Accounts Contradict These Scriptures

However, this contradicts empirical evidence. We have all experienced petitions presented to God that were denied. Even Scripture provides examples of denied petitions. Consider, for example:

- David pled that God not take the life of his son (2Sa 12:16), but the child died after seven days of illness (2Sa 12:18)).
- In his anger (Jon 4:1), Jonah prayed to the Lord, saying, "please take my life from me, for it is better for me to

die than to live!" (Jon 4:3). The Lord denied Jonah's petition.

- Paul pled with God three times regarding his "thorn": "Concerning this thing I pleaded with the Lord three times that it might depart from me. And He said to me, 'My grace is sufficient for you, for My strength is made perfect in weakness.' Therefore most gladly I will rather boast in my infirmities, that the power of Christ may rest upon me" (2Co 12:8-9).

- Jesus prayed, saying "Father, if it is Your will, take this cup away from Me," but He added, "nevertheless not My will, but Yours, be done" (Luk 22:42). The cup was not taken from Him; it was God's plan that Jesus go to be crucified.

II. PROPOSED EXPLANATION

1. Introduction: Other Scriptures Provide the Necessary Context and Explanation

We have to understand the referenced Scriptures in light of their context and in light of other Scripture, which teach that prayers are answered only when the following conditions are met:

- We ask with faith that the things we say will be done and do not doubt in our hearts (Mat 21:21-22; Mark 11:23-24; Jam 1:6);

- The petition is in accordance with God's will (1 John 5:14-15). We can know God's will by abiding in Him (John 15:7);

- We ask in Jesus' Name (John 14:12-14);

- The petition is free of worldly lust, for if we lust, we do not receive (Jam 4:2-3). It is not enough that the petition be free of worldly lust; the motivation also must be pure and free of lust (e.g., seeking spiritual gifts to edify others, not for egotistic reasons);

- We must first eliminate sin, unrighteousness and lack of forgiveness from our lives. Our sins can separate us from God, so that He will not hear (Isa 59:2-3), but the fervent prayer of the righteous is effective (Jam 5:16-18). Jesus also commands that before praying, we must first forgive our brothers and sisters (Mark 11:25-26).

2. Ask in Faith (Mat 21:21-22; Mark 11:23-24; Jam 1:6)

From other Scripture, we learn that asking in faith is a condition to answered prayer:

- "[I]f you have faith and do not doubt, you will not only do what was done to the fig tree, but also if you say to this mountain, 'Be removed and be cast into the sea,' it will be done. And whatever things you ask in prayer, believing, you will receive" (Mat 21:21-22).
- "[W]hoever says to this mountain, 'Be removed and be cast into the sea,' and does not doubt in his heart, but believes that those things he says will be done, he will have whatever he says. Therefore I say to you, whatever things you ask when you pray, believe that you receive them, and you will have them" (Mark 11:23-24).
- "Let him ask in *faith*, with *no doubting*, for he who doubts is like a wave of the sea driven and tossed by the wind" (Jam 1:6).

3. Ask for God's Will (1 John 5:14-15)

In addition, we must ask for God's will.

a. Overview: When Our Petition Does Not Align with God's Will

It is possible that what we petition of God is not in accordance with His will. Paul pled with God three times regarding his "thorn," but God said to him, "My grace is sufficient for you" (2Co 12:8-9), and the petition was denied. Similarly, Jesus prayed that God take away the "cup" of his Passion and His suffering (Luk 22:42), but the cup was not taken from Him. If it was possible that Jesus or Paul would petition God for something that was not of God's will, then certainly it is possible that we too might petition God for something that is not of His will.

b. Scriptural Basis

As referenced earlier, Matthew 7:7 and Luke 11:9 imply that whatever we ask will be given to us.

However, 1 John 5:14-15 makes it clear that it is the petitions that are made *according to God's will* that are granted. Consider:

> "Now this is the confidence that we have in Him, that if we ask anything according to *His will*, He hears us. And if we know that He hears us, whatever we ask, we know that we have the petitions that we have asked of Him" (1Jn 5:14-15).

In this same vein, our petitions are granted when we abide in God:

> "If you abide in Me, and My words abide in you, you will ask what you desire, and it shall be done for you" (John 15:7).

c. Petitions Asked for in Worldly Lust Are Not Granted (Jam 4:2-3)

James writes:

> "You lust and do not have. You murder and covet and cannot obtain. You fight and war. Yet you do not have because you do not ask. You ask and do not receive, because you ask amiss, that you may spend it on your pleasures" (Jam 4:2-3).

This does not necessarily mean that what the person is asking for is wrong; a person may petition God for something that in itself is not wrong but may be doing so for the wrong reasons.

James then admonishes:

> "Adulterers and adulteresses! Do you not know that friendship with the world is enmity with God? Whoever therefore wants to be a friend of the world makes himself an enemy of God" (Jam 4:2-4)

This, reinforces the fact that much of what we ask for may in fact be friendship with the world (in the form of wealth, power, etc.), which ultimately drives us away from God.

d. God Grants What Is Good for His Children

Because God only grants what is good for his children, He only grants those petitions that are in accordance with His Will. Otherwise, we would be able to ask for what is detrimental to us (*e.g.*, an adulterous relationship) and it would be granted, though the thing granted might be harmful to us and contrary to God's will.

In the two "Scriptures to Consider" above (Mat 7:7-8 and Luke 11:9-10), if we continue reading, it becomes clear that God grants us petitions in accordance with His will (*i.e.*, that are for our good). Mat 7 continues:

> "Which of you, if his son requests bread, gives him a stone (Mat 7:9)? Or if he requests a fish, gives him a snake (Mat 7:10)? If you give good things to your children, *then how much more will your heavenly father give good things to those who petition him* (Mat 7:11)?"

Similarly, Luke 11 continues:

> "Which of you will give a stone to his son, who asks for bread? Or for a fish, will give him a snake? Or for an egg, will give him a scorpion (Luke 11:11-12)? If then you who are evil give good things to your children, how much more will your heavenly father give the Holy Spirit to those who ask (Luke 11:13)?"

While these passages make clear that God gives liberally to His children what is good for them, they do not imply that he necessarily gives everything requested. What is clear is that God gives according to His will (*i.e.*, what is good for his children).

e.   God May Have Something Better in Mind

God declares: "my thoughts are not your thoughts, neither are your ways my ways" (Isa 55:8). The Lord may deny our requests only to give us something much better, for He "is able to do exceedingly abundantly above all that we ask or think" (Eph 3:20). Thus, we may be unable to even think about or fathom what God has planned. While we plan for our lives and future, He may have something else in store that requires denying what we have asked for so that a much better plan comes about.

4. Ask in Jesus' Name (John 14:12-14)

"Most assuredly, I say to you, he who believes in Me, the works that I do he will do also; and greater works than these he will do, because I go to My Father. And whatever you ask **in My name**, that I will do, that the Father may be glorified in the Son. If you ask anything **in My name**, I will do it" (John 14:12-14).

5. Eliminate Sin, Unrighteousness and Lack of Forgiveness from Our Lives (Pro 28:13; Isa 59:2-3; Jam 5:16-18; Mark 11:25-26)

Sin, unrighteousness and lack of forgiveness separate us from God and can have an impact on the effectiveness of our prayer.

a.   Sin and Unrighteousness

Consider:

- Confess your trespasses to one another, and pray for one another, that you may be healed. The effective, fervent prayer of a righteous man avails much. Elijah was a man with a nature like ours, and he prayed earnestly that it would not rain; and it did not rain on the land for three years and six months. And he prayed again, and the heaven gave rain, and the earth produced its fruit (Jam 5:16-18).

In contrast:

- "Behold, the Lord's hand is not shortened, That it cannot save; Nor His ear heavy, That it cannot hear. But your iniquities have separated you from your God; And your sins have hidden His face from you, So that He will not hear. For your hands are defiled with blood, And your fingers with iniquity; Your lips have spoken lies, Your tongue has muttered perversity" (Isa 59:1-3).

- "He who covers his sins will not prosper, But whoever confesses and forsakes them will have mercy" (Pro 28:13).

b. Lack of Forgiveness

When praying, we must first forgive our trespassers:

"And whenever you stand praying, if you have anything against anyone, forgive him, that your Father in heaven may also forgive you your trespasses. But if you do not forgive, neither will your Father in heaven forgive your trespasses" (Mark 11:25-26).

III. CONCLUSION

1. Abide in God

We should therefore first seek God's will because whenever "we ask anything according to His will, He hears us" (1Jn 5:14). We should "abide" in God, so that whatever we ask "shall be done for you" (John 15:7).

2. All Things Work Together for Good for Those Who Love God

Moreover, we should trust that "[a]ll things work together for good to those who love God, to those who are the called according to His purpose" (Rom 8:28). Paul writes that we should "Be anxious for nothing, but in everything by prayer and supplication, with thanksgiving, let your requests be made known to God; and the peace of God, which surpasses all understanding, will guard your hearts and minds through Christ Jesus" (Php 4:6-7). While it is true that not all of our petitions are granted, Paul nonetheless instructs us to continue to make supplication "in everything" (Php 4:6).

CHAPTER 4. ARE WE JUDGED BY FAITH OR WORKS?

I. WE ARE JUDGED ACCORDING TO OUR WORKS

Romans 2 states:

Rom 2:5 But in accordance with your hardness and your impenitent heart you are treasuring up for yourself wrath in the day of wrath and revelation of the righteous judgment of God,

Rom 2:6 who *"WILL RENDER TO EACH ONE ACCORDING TO HIS DEEDS"*:

Rom 2:7 eternal life to those who by patient continuance in doing good seek for glory, honor, and immortality;

Rom 2:8 but to those who are self-seeking and do not obey the truth, but obey unrighteousness--indignation and wrath,

Rom 2:9 *tribulation and anguish, on every soul of man who does evil, of the Jew first and also of the Greek*;

Rom 2:10 but *glory, honor, and peace to everyone who works what is good*, to the Jew first and also to the Greek.

Rom 2:11 For there is no partiality with God.

Rom 2:12 For as many as have sinned without law will also perish without law, and as many as have sinned in the law will be judged by the law

Rom 2:13 (for not the hearers of the law are just in the sight of God, but *the doers of the law will be justified*;

II. WE ARE JUSTIFIED BY FAITH

However, Romans 3 states:

Rom 3:28 Therefore we conclude that a man is justified by faith apart from the deeds of the law.

Romans 5 states:

Rom 5:1 Therefore, having been justified by faith, we have peace with God through our Lord Jesus Christ,

Rom 5:2 through whom also we have access by faith into this grace in which we stand, and rejoice in hope of the glory of God.

III. RESOLUTION

Romans 2:6, which states that God "will render to each one according to his deeds," is referring to the default under sin and nature. Man is judged by his deeds. Because "all have sinned and fall short of the glory of God" (Rom 3:23), all receive condemnation by default. However, Romans 3 and 5 describe an alternate route to salvation. This second route is not based on a person's deeds, but on the perfect deed of Christ in fulfilling the law at Calvary. Through faith in Christ, a person is justified "apart from the deeds of the law" (Rom 3:28). "Having been justified by faith, we have peace with God through our Lord Jesus Christ" (Rom 5:1).

Romans 2 needs to be read in the context of the entire book of Romans, which makes clear in Chapters 3, 4 and 5 that righteousness comes through faith, for all are sinners apart from faith in God:

- Romans 3 teaches that the righteousness of God, apart from the law, has been made known by the Law and the Prophets (Rom 3:21). *This righteousness is given through faith in Jesus Christ to all who believe* (Rom 3:22). While all have sinned and fall short of the glory of God (Rom 3:23), all are justified freely by his grace through the redemption that came by Christ (Rom 3:24).
- Romans 4 states that it was not through the law that Abraham and his offspring received the promise that he would be an heir, but through the righteousness that comes by faith (Rom 4:13).
- Romans 5 states that "having been justified by faith, we have peace with God through our Lord Jesus Christ, through whom also we have access by faith into this

grace in which we stand, and rejoice in hope of the glory of God (Rom 5:1-2).

CHAPTER 5. DID 40,000 HORSEMEN OR 40,000 FOOT SOLDIERS DIE IN BATTLE WITH DAVID?

I. OVERVIEW

The author of 2 Samuel states that 40,000 <u>horsemen</u> died during a battle with David, while the author of 1 Chronicles states that 40,000 <u>foot soldiers</u> died:

> 2Sa 10:18 Then the Syrians fled before Israel; and David killed seven hundred charioteers and <u>forty thousand horsemen</u> of the Syrians, and struck Shobach the commander of their army, who died there.
>
> 1Ch 19:18 Then the Syrians fled before Israel; and David killed seven thousand charioteers and <u>forty thousand foot soldiers</u> of the Syrians, and killed Shophach the commander of the army.

II. PROPOSED EXPLANATION

It is entirely conceivable that the 40,000 horsemen were also foot soldiers. Therefore, 40,000 horsemen / foot soldiers perished. Alternatively, it is possible that 40,000 horsemen *and* 40,000 foot soldiers, for a total of 80,000, perished.

CHAPTER 6. DID BOTH THIEVES OR ONLY ONE THIEF MOCK JESUS ON THE CROSS?

I. OVERVIEW

1. According to Matthew, Both Thieves Mocked Jesus

Mat 27:38 Then two thieves were put on crosses with him, one on the right and one on the left.

…

Mat 27:44 And the thieves who were on the crosses said evil words to him.

2. According to Mark, Both Thieves Mocked Jesus

Mark 15:27 And they put two thieves on crosses with him, one on his right side, and one on his left.

…

Mark 15:32 Let the Christ, the King of Israel, come down now from the cross, so that we may see and have belief. And those who were put on crosses with him said evil things against him.

…

Mark 15:37 And Jesus gave a loud cry, and gave up his spirit.

3. According to Luke, Only One Thief Mocked Jesus

Luke 23:32 And two others, evil-doers, were taken with him to be put to death.

Luke 23:33 And when they came to the place which is named Golgotha, they put him on the cross, and the evil-doers, one on the right side, and the other on the left.

Luke 23:34 And Jesus said, Father, let them have forgiveness, for they have no knowledge of what they are doing.

And they made division of his clothing among them by the decision of chance.

...

Luke 23:39 And one of the evil-doers on the cross, with bitter feeling, said to him, Are you not the Christ? Get yourself and us out of this.

Luke 23:40 But the other, protesting, said, Have you no fear of God? for you have a part in the same punishment,

Luke 23:41 And with reason; for we have the right reward of our acts, but this man has done nothing wrong.

Luke 23:42 And he said, Jesus, keep me in mind when you come in your kingdom.

Luke 23:43 And he said to him, Truly I say to you, Today you will be with me in Paradise.

4. John does not Specify

John 19:23 And when Jesus was nailed to the cross, the men of the army took his clothing, and made a division of it into four parts, to every man a part, and they took his coat: now the coat was without a join, made out of one bit of cloth.

...

John 19:25 Now by the side of the cross of Jesus were his mother, and his mother's sister Mary, the wife of Cleopas, and Mary Magdalene.

John 19:26 So when Jesus saw his mother and the disciple who was dear to him, he said to his mother, Mother, there is your son!

John 19:27 Then he said to the disciple, There is your mother! And from that hour the disciple took her to his house.

...

John 19:30 So when Jesus had taken the wine he said, All is done. And with his head bent he gave up his spirit.

II. POSSIBLE EXPLANATION

Jesus was crucified between two thieves. It is possible that both of them initially mocked Jesus. However, one of them, when he saw the loving response of Jesus, realized that Jesus was who He claimed to be and repented on the cross.

Jesus remained on the cross for at least three hours, which would have left enough time for the good thief's repentance.

While the accounts of Matthew and Mark, on the one hand, and Luke, on the other, are not identical, it is possible that they could be reconciled to one another by taking into account that the two are accounts from different perspectives.

CHAPTER 7. DID GOD OR SATAN PROVOKE DAVID TO TAKE THE CENSUS?

I. OVERVIEW

According to 2 Samuel, God moved David to take a census of Israel. However, according to 1 Chronicles, Satan moved David to take a census.

2 Samuel Account	1 Chronicles Account
2Sa 24:1 Again the anger of the <u>Lord</u> was aroused against Israel, and <u>He moved David</u> against them to say, "Go, number Israel and Judah."	1Ch 21:1 Now <u>Satan</u> stood up against Israel, and <u>moved David</u> to number Israel.
2Sa 24:2 So the king said to Joab the commander of the army who was with him, "Now go throughout all the tribes of Israel, from Dan to Beersheba, and count the people, that I may know the number of the people."	1Ch 21:2 So David said to Joab and to the leaders of the people, "Go, number Israel from Beersheba to Dan, and bring the number of them to me that I may know it."

II. PROPOSED EXPLANATION

1. Overview

What likely happened here is Satan directly provoked David directly (1 Chronicles 21:1), but God gave Satan permission to do so, as we see in the book of Job. In Job, Satan presents himself before the Lord and requests God's permission to afflict his faithful servant, Job. Satan insists that Job only serves God because of His blessings, and he would surely curse God if he were tested. God conditionally grants Satan's request.[1]

2. Author Perspectives

We should also consider the emphases of the respective authors of 2 Samuel (probably Nathan or Gad), who viewed the affair in the sense of God's ultimate control over all things, and the author of 1 Chronicles (probably Ezra), who emphasized the satanic plot and how God used it as a tool for judgment. That 2 Samuel focuses on God as the mover finds support in the fact that Nathan and Gad were prophets who proclaimed God's control over the affairs of men. Ezra, in contrast, was a priest interested in pointing out the holiness of God and who hates sin.[2]

It would thus appear that the account of who moved David to number of Israel varies based on each author's respective purpose. The author of 2 Samuel states that "the anger of the Lord was aroused against Israel" (2Sa 24:1). The author thus wishes to emphasize that granting leave to Satan to move David to count Israel and Judah was used by God to bring judgment on Israel with one of the three choices offered to David (three (seven) years of famine, fleeing three months before David's enemies or three days' of plague) (2Sa 24:13). The author of 2 Samuel thus states that it was the Lord who moved David to number Israel and Judah in order to link this with the Lord's anger against Israel and the ensuring judgment brought upon Israel. The author of 2 Chronicles, in contrast, does not mention the Lord's anger up front. The Lord's anger only comes up after Joab gave the sum to David: "God was displeased with this thing; therefore He struck Israel" (1Ch 21:7).

Therefore, recognizing that God's greater purpose in moving David to number Israel and Judah was to bring judgment on Israel, the author of 2 Samuel mentions that it was God who moved David. The author of 2 Chronicles, in contrast,

---

[1] Taken from https://www.premier.org.uk/Topics/Church/Apologetics/Who-moved-King-David-to-number-Israel.
[2] See https://answersingenesis.org/contradictions-in-the-bible/contradiction-who-incited-david-to-count-the-fighting-men-of-israel/.

not seeking to draw attention to this point, references only Satan, who was used by God as an agent to bring about God's greater purpose. In both cases, David's act was used to bring judgment on Israel.

3. God's Greater Purpose in Moving David to Number Israel

God's greater purpose in moving David to number Israel was to bring punishment upon Israel, for "[a]gain the anger of the Lord was aroused against Israel." The previous occasion may have been the famine of 2 Samuel 21:

> 2Sa 21:1 Now there was a famine in the days of David for three years, year after year; and David inquired of the Lord. And the Lord answered, "It is because of Saul and his bloodthirsty house, because he killed the Gibeonites."
> 2Sa 21:2 So the king called the Gibeonites and spoke to them. Now the Gibeonites were not of the children of Israel, but of the remnant of the Amorites; the children of Israel had sworn protection to them, but Saul had sought to kill them in his zeal for the children of Israel and Judah.

The specific reason for God's anger against Israel in 2 Samuel 24 is not stated. However, it is clear that God's anger is directed against Israel, not David. According to the *NIV Study Bible*, His anger may have been based on the Israelite's support among for the rebellions of Absalom and Sheba against David, the divinely chosen and anointed king (see 2 Samuel 24:1 footnote). God thus moved David to number Israel in order to punish Israel for their wrongdoing and in turn draw Israel back to Himself.

4. God Can Use Satan as an Agent to Bring About His Plan

When a principal uses an agent to enter into and sign agreements on his behalf, it can be said that the principal entered into the agreements, even though it was the agent that actually signed, because the agent is acting as a representative of the principal. Similarly, if the agent undertakes any authorized act, the principal is bound by that act, not because the principal undertook the act, but because his authorized agent did so.

So too is it with God and his creation. God can use Satan and man to effect his ultimate purposes. If God uses Satan to effect His ultimate plan, it can be said that God undertook the act, even though it was Satan actually acting, because God acts as the principal over all of creation.

We see examples of God using Satan to accomplish His purposes throughout scripture:

- In Job, Satan was required to obtain God's permission before tormenting Job. Similarly, we see in various places in the Scripture that God is said to harden someone's heart, and the person also hardens his own heart. Because God is sovereign over everything, he can allow man or the Satan to work evil, which God can then use in His own plans for good.
- In the New Testament, Jesus told Simon Peter that Satan desired to sift him as wheat (Luke 22:31), to which Jesus consented, but only for a greater purpose.
- God allowed Satan to put a "thorn" in Paul's flesh, lest Paul "be exalted above measure" (2Co 12:7).
- God sent a "distressing" spirit to King Saul (1Sa 16:14), likely to chastise him for his disobedience.
- God sent a spirit of ill will between Abimelech and the men of Shechem (Jdg 9:23) to bring judgment on Abimelech for his sin.
- God allowed a spirit to "go out and be a lying spirit in the mouth of all [of Ahab's] prophets," so that Ahab would fall in battle at Ramoth Gilead (1Ki 22:20-22).
- Paul instructed the church to deliver a sinful man to Satan (i.e., cast him out of the church or, according to some interpretations, allow Satan to bring physical affliction to the man) "for the destruction of the flesh, that his spirit may be saved in the day of the Lord Jesus" (1Co 5:5).

We should thus read the 2 Samuel 24:1 account as stating that God *indirectly* moved David to number Israel by granting Satan leave to do so, in the same way that he granted Satan leave to afflict Job, in order to realize God's greater purpose. In other words, God used Satan as an agent.

III. PROBLEMS WITH PROPOSED EXPLANATION

1. 2 Samuel Clearly States that Satan Moved David to Take a Census, Not That Satan Did So with God's Permission

a. Overview

The problem with the proposed explanation is that neither 2 Samuel nor 1 Chronicles state that Satan requested God's permission to provoke David or that God permitted Satan to do so. Instead, 2 Samuel 24:1 clearly states that God "moved David" to take a census, but 1 Chronicles 21:1 clearly states that Satan "moved David" to take a census.

b. Response

a. God Granted Satan Permission to Move David

The apparent contradiction can be reconciled by viewing Satan as being used by God as God's agent to directly move David, while God acted indirectly in moving David by granting Satan permission to move Satan. While the scripture does not explicitly provide this principal/agent framework, it is important to recall that just because the Bible does not state that something occurred does not mean that it did not occur. Not every detail of every historical event is recounted in the Bible. The extinction of the dinosaurs, the birth of the prophet Elijah and Hitler's invasion of Poland are all events that occurred but that are not reported in the Bible. Just because they are not reported does not mean they did not occur.

It is thus entirely possible that Satan directly provoked David directly (1 Chronicles 21:1), but God gave Satan permission to do so, as we see in the book of Job. However, the 2 Samuel account simply states that God moved David to number Israel, without mentioning the detail that he was doing so indirectly by granting Satan leave to do so, while the 1

Chronicles account states that Satan moved David to number Israel. 1 Samuel does not state that Satan did this, as with all things, with the leave of God.

b.   God Does Not Cause Sin, but Even Evil Acts Are under God's Control

"Let no one say when he is tempted, 'I am tempted by God'; for God cannot be tempted by evil, nor does He Himself tempt anyone. But each one is tempted when he is drawn away by his own desires and enticed" (Jam 1:13-15).

However, even evil acts are under God's sovereign control. Consider:

- God hardened Pharaoh's heart:
    o "And the Lord said to Moses, 'When you go back to Egypt, see that you do all those wonders before Pharaoh which I have put in your hand. But I will harden his heart, so that he will not let the people go'" (Exo 4:21);
    o "Pharaoh's heart grew hard, and he did not heed them, as the Lord had said" (Exo 7:13);
    o "But the Lord hardened the heart of Pharaoh; and he did not heed them, just as the Lord had spoken to Moses" (Exo 9:12)
    o "Now the Lord said to Moses, 'Go in to Pharaoh; for I have hardened his heart and the hearts of his servants, that I may show these signs of Mine before him'" (Exo 10:1);
    o "But the Lord hardened Pharaoh's heart, and he did not let the children of Israel go" (Exo 10:20);
    o "But the Lord hardened Pharaoh's heart, and he would not let them go" (Exo 10:27);
    o "So Moses and Aaron did all these wonders before Pharaoh; and the Lord hardened Pharaoh's heart, and he did not let the children of Israel go out of his land" (Exo 11:10);
    o "Then I will harden Pharaoh's heart, so that he will pursue them; and I will gain honor over Pharaoh and over all his army, that the Egyptians may know that I am the Lord" (Exo 14:4).

- "There was not a city that made peace with the children of Israel, except the Hivites, the inhabitants of Gibeon. All the others they took in battle. For it was of the Lord to harden their hearts, that they should come against Israel in battle, that He might utterly destroy them, and that they might receive no mercy, but that He might destroy them, as the Lord had commanded Moses" (Jos 11:19-20)

- "And the Lord said, 'Who will persuade Ahab to go up, that he may fall at Ramoth Gilead?' So one spoke in this manner, and another spoke in that manner. Then a spirit came forward and stood before the Lord, and said, 'I will persuade him.' The Lord said to him, 'In what way?' So he said, 'I will go out and be a lying spirit in the mouth of all his prophets.' And the Lord said, 'You shall persuade him, and also prevail. Go out and do so.' Therefore look! The Lord has put a lying spirit in the mouth of all these prophets of yours, and the Lord has declared disaster against you" (1Ki 22:20-23).

- Job 1:12 And the Lord said to Satan, "Behold, all that he has is in your power; only do not lay a hand on his person" (Job 1:12).

c. God's Use of Satan to Bring About Justice

God ultimately wishes good upon creation. His thoughts are "of peace and not of evil, to give you a future and a hope" (Jer 29:11). He "desires all men to be saved and to come to the knowledge of the truth" (1Ti 2:4). God is also just. He "will not pervert justice" (Job 34:12); "all His ways are justice" and he is a "God of truth and without injustice" (Deu 32:4), one who "love[s] justice" (Isa 61:8). In bringing about His perfect plan, God can use Satan and man. He can use them in bringing about justice, as we see in 1 Chronicles, as well as to bring about mercy.

2. It Does Not Seem Logical that God would Use David's Numbering of Israel to Punish Israel Rather than Punish Israel Directly

a. Overview

Using David's numbering of Israel to punish Israel for the rebellions of Absalom and Sheba appears to be somewhat convoluted. If Israel sinned and rebelled against God, one would expect God to punish Israel directly for their sin. It is unclear why God would first move David to sin and then use that to punish Israel for their sin.

b. Response

It is possible that God was testing David to see what was inside his heart, particularly pride, and whether he would put his trust in his men rather than in God. It is thus possible that God allowed Satan to tempt David to number Israel, and David succumbed. In other words, God used Satan to entice David and when David succumbed, the pride that David had in his heart came to light, prompting David to remorse and repentance. God used the tempting of David to accomplish the dual purpose of testing David while simultaneously bringing punishment upon Israel   for   their   rebellion.

CHAPTER 8. DID JESUS COME TO BRING PEACE?

I. OVERVIEW

Some verses suggest Jesus came to bring peace:

- "For unto us a Child is born, unto us a Son is given; and the government will be upon His shoulder. And His name will be called Wonderful, Counselor, Mighty God, Everlasting Father, Prince of Peace" (Isa 9:6).
- "Peace I leave with you; My peace I give to you; not as the world gives, do I give to you. Let not your heart be troubled, nor let it be fearful" (John 14:27).
- "These things I have spoken to you, that in Me you may have peace" (John 16:33).
- "The word which He sent to the sons of Israel, preaching peace through Jesus Christ (He is Lord of all)" (Acts 10:36).
- "Now all things are of God, who has reconciled us to Himself through Jesus Christ, and has given us the ministry of reconciliation" (2Co 5:18).

Other verses suggest Jesus did not come to bring peace:

- "Do not think that I came to bring peace on the earth; I did not come to bring peace, but a sword. For I came to set a man against his father, and a daughter against her mother, and a daughter-in-law against her mother-in-law; and a man's enemies will be the members of his household" (Matthew 10:34-36).
- "Do you suppose that I came to give peace on earth? I tell you, not at all, but rather division. For from now on five in one house will be divided: three against two, and two against three. Father will be divided against son and son against father, mother against daughter and daughter

against mother, mother-in-law against her daughter-in-law and daughter-in-law against her mother-in-law" (Luke 12:51-53).

- "But now, let him who has a purse take it along, likewise also a bag, and let him who has no sword sell his robe and buy one" (Luke 22:36).

II. RESOLUTION

In fact, Jesus is the Prince of Peace (Isa 9:6), who came to bring reconciliation between God and man (2Co 5:18).

The references to the sword that Jesus makes in the Gospels of Matthew and Luke should not be read as a contradiction to this, but rather, as figurative speech indicating the division and conflict that the Gospel brings between Christ's followers and His enemies, between believers and unbelievers, sometimes even within the same family.

Also, Jesus' reference to the "sword" in Luke 22:36 is not meant to be interpreted literally. It is a figure of speech referencing the perils that would soon face Jesus' followers. Yet Jesus never taught self-defense by the sword. In fact, when Peter cut off the high priest's servant's ear at Jesus' arrest at Gethsemane, Jesus instructed him to put away his sword (John 18:10-11). Rather, Jesus taught not to resist an evil person, but to turn the other cheek (Mat 5:39).

CHAPTER 9. DID JUDAS ISCARIOT DIE BY HANGING OR DID HE DIE BY FALLING AND BURSTING OPEN?

I. OVERVIEW

Matthew 27:5 states that Judas Iscariot died by hanging, but Acts 1:18 states he died by falling and bursting open:

- Mat 27:5 Then he threw down the pieces of silver in the temple and departed, and went and hanged himself.
- Acts 1:18 Now this man purchased a field with the wages of iniquity; and falling headlong, he burst open in the middle and all his entrails gushed out.

II. PROPOSED EXPLANATION

Matthew's Gospel account and Luke's account in Acts are two different viewpoints of the same event:

- Matthew tells us that Judas died by hanging.
- Luke, being a doctor, gives us a graphic description of what occurred following the hanging (*i.e.*, Judas fell, burst open and his organs spilled.

It is possible that Judas hanged himself and he fell down, with his entrails spilling out. Most likely, if a person falls and his entrails spill out, he will probably not survive the event. However, if a person hangs himself, he might survive the event (e.g., in the event he rescues himself by climbing up the robe or untying it, or in the event the rope or branch on which he is hung snaps before the person dies). Therefore, Judas likely hanged himself before he fell and had his entrails spill. While it is possible that Judas could have survived the hanging and then fell, what is more likely is that while he was hanging, he fell following a break in the rope or the branch from which he hung breaking). The fact that he could have hanged himself before falling from the rope indicates that the apparent discrepancies between the accounts in Matthew and Luke are not necessarily contradictions.

CHAPTER 10. EACH PERSON DIES FOR HIS OWN SIN, YET JESUS, WHO WAS INNOCENT, DIED FOR SINNERS

I. EACH PERSON DIES FOR HIS OWN SIN

- "[E]very one shall die for his own iniquity; every man who eats the sour grapes, his teeth shall be set on edge" (Jer 31:30).
- "The soul who sins shall die" (Eze 18:4) ... "The righteousness of the righteous shall be upon himself, and the wickedness of the wicked shall be upon himself" (Eze 18:20).

II. JESUS, WHO WAS INNOCENT, DIED FOR SINNERS

- "God so loved the world that He gave His only begotten Son, that whoever believes in Him should not perish but have everlasting life" (John 3:16).

III. CONTRADICTION

There appears to be a contradiction in these verses. On the one hand, Jeremiah and Ezekiel affirm that God's judgment applies to each individual according to his own sins, not those of, for example, his father or child. A righteous person brings righteousness upon himself and a wicked person brings wickedness upon himself. One who acts righteously shall live (Eze 18:17) and one who does iniquity shall die (Eze 18:18).

Yet Jesus, who was innocent and without blemish (1Pe 1:19), died a sinner's death. Sinners, who deserve death (Rom 6:23), are given life through Jesus (John 3:16).

If God's law in Jeremiah and Ezekiel is applied, then should not every man die, since every man is a sinner (Rom 3:23) and the wages of sin is death (Rom 6:23)?

IV. ANSWER

God's law implements a system justice in which death is the consequence of sin (Rom 6:23).

At the same time, God tempers His justice with grace, which is expressed through forgiveness.

Under God's law, a sinner is to be put to death (Rom 6:23). Through His grace, God allows a sinner to substitute his death with that of an animal, offered to God as a sacrifice, as there is no forgiveness without the shedding of blood (Heb 9:22).

Animal sacrifice for sin atonement was established in the Mosaic law: Leviticus details the nature of the sacrifice that was to be made as an "atonement" to bring forgiveness of sin (Lev 4:33-35). Yet it may even go as far back as the Garden of Eden: God made for Adam and Eve "tunics of skin" (Gen 3:21), which implies that God put to death an animal, perhaps to cover not only Adam and Eve's shame, but also their sin.

Whereas the Israelites were able to experience God's forgiveness through animal sacrifice under His law, even for sins as serious as idolatry (Hos 14:3), other peoples, such as the Amelkites, were systematically wiped away for their sin (1Sa 15:1-3).

The crucifixion of Christ is then to be characterized as one final, perfect sacrifice (Heb 9:26), the realization of Old Testament substitute sacrifice for atonement. Animal sacrifices foreshadowed and mirrored Jesus' sacrifice on our behalf, but it was imperfect in that it required constant repetition and did not transform the sinner into a new creature.

CHAPTER 11. GENEALOGY OF JESUS CHRIST

I. INTRODUCTION

1. Overview

Dr. Philips writes (p. 27-28):

When the genealogy of Jesus from David in Matthew 1:6-16 is compared to that of Luke 3:23-31, there are major discrepancies. Firstly, Jesus in Matthew has 26 parents between himself and David, but in Luke he has 41. Secondly, the names in both lists vary radically after David, and only two names are the same: Joseph, and Zorobabel. Both lists start off with Joseph, strangely enough, as the father of Jesus, but in Matthew, the author records Jesus' paternal grandfather as being Jacob, while in Luke he is Heli. If one were to accept the suggestion of some that one of the lists is actually the genealogy of Mary, it could not possibly account for any differences after their common ancestor David. Both lists meet again at Abraham and between David and Abraham most of the names are the same. However, in Matthew's list, Hezron's son's name is Ram, the father of Ammin'adab, while in Luke's list, Hezron's son's name is Ami whose son's name is Admin, the father of Ammin'adab.45 Consequently, between David and Abraham there are 12 forefathers in Matthew's list and 13 in Luke's list. T Visits to Jesus' Tomb Following the Crucifixion

2. Matthew's Account

Matthew's account of the genealogy is as follows (Mat 1:2-16):

- Mat 1:2 Abraham begot Isaac
- Isaac begot Jacob
- **Jacob** begot Judah and his brothers
- Mat 1:3 Judah begot Perez and Zerah by Tamar

- Perez begot Hezron
- Hezron begot Ram
- Mat 1:4 Ram begot Amminadab[3]
- Amminadab begot Nahshon
- Nahshon begot Salmon
- Mat 1:5 Salmon begot Boaz by Rahab
- Boaz begot Obed by Ruth
- Obed begot Jesse
- Mat 1:6 and Jesse begot *David* the king
- *David* the king begot Solomon by her who had been the wife of Uriah.
- Mat 1:7 Solomon begot Rehoboam
- Rehoboam begot Abijah
- Abijah begot Asa
- Mat 1:8 Asa begot Jehoshaphat
- Jehoshaphat begot Joram
- Joram begot Uzziah
- Mat 1:9 Uzziah begot Jotham
- Jotham begot Ahaz
- Ahaz begot Hezekiah
- Mat 1:10 Hezekiah begot Manasseh
- Manasseh begot Amon
- Amon begot Josiah
- Mat 1:11 Josiah begot Jeconiah and his brothers about the time they were carried away to *Babylon*
- Mat 1:12 And after they were brought to *Babylon*, Jeconiah begot Shealtiel
- Shealtiel begot Zerubbabel
- Mat 1:13 Zerubbabel begot Abiud
- Abiud begot Eliakim
- Eliakim begot Azor
- Mat 1:14 Azor begot Zadok
- Zadok begot Achim
- Achim begot Eliud
- Mat 1:15 Eliud begot Eleazar
- Eleazar begot Matthan
- Matthan begot Jacob

---

[3] Amminadab was likely a contemporary of Moses.

- Mat 1:16 Jacob begot Joseph the husband of Mary
- of whom was born Jesus who is called Christ.
- Mat 1:17 So all the generations from Abraham to David are *fourteen generations*, from David until the captivity in Babylon are *fourteen generations*, and from the captivity in Babylon until the Christ are *fourteen generations*.

3. Luke's Account (Luke 3:23-38)

Luke's account of the genealogy of Christ is as follows:

- Luke 3:23 Now Jesus Himself began His ministry at about thirty years of age, being (as was supposed) the son of Joseph
- *the son* of Heli,
- Luke 3:24 the son of Matthat
- the son of Levi
- the son of Melchi
- the son of Janna
- the son of Joseph,
- Luke 3:25 the son of Mattathiah
- the son of Amos
- the son of Nahum
- the son of Esli
- the son of Naggai
- Luke 3:26 the son of Maath
- the son of Mattathiah
- the son of Semei
- the son of Joseph
- the son of Judah,
- Luke 3:27 the son of Joannas
- the son of Rhesa
- the son of Zerubbabel
- the son of Shealtiel
- the son of Neri
- Luke 3:28 the son of Melchi
- the son of Addi
- the son of Cosam
- the son of Elmodam

- the son of Er
- Luke 3:29 the son of Jose
- the son of Eliezer
- the son of Jorim
- the son of Matthat
- the son of Levi
- Luke 3:30 the son of Simeon
- the son of Judah
- the son of Joseph
- the son of Jonan
- the son of Eliakim
- Luke 3:31 the son of Melea
- the son of Menan
- the son of Mattathah
- the son of Nathan
- the son of David
- Luke 3:32 the son of Jesse
- the son of Obed
- the son of Boaz
- the son of Salmon
- the son of Nahshon
- Luke 3:33 the son of Amminadab
- the son of Ram
- the son of Hezron
- the son of Perez
- the son of Judah
- Luke 3:34 the son of Jacob
- the son of Isaac
- the son of Abraham
- the son of Terah
- the son of Nahor
- Luke 3:35 the son of Serug
- the son of Reu
- the son of Peleg
- the son of Eber
- the son of Shelah
- Luke 3:36 the son of Cainan
- the son of Arphaxad
- the son of Shem
- the son of Noah

- the son of Lamech
- Luke 3:37 the son of Methuselah
- the son of Enoch
- the son of Jared
- the son of Mahalalel
- the son of Cainan
- Luke 3:38 the son of Enosh
- the son of Seth
- the son of Adam
- the son of God.

4. Comparison

Matthew 1:2-16	*Luke (3:23-38)*
	God
	Adam
	Seth
	Enosh
	Cainan
	Mahalalel
	Jared
	Enoch
	Methuselah
	Lamech
	Noah
	Shem
	Arphaxad
	Cainan
	Shelah
	Eber
	Peleg
	Reu
	Luke 3:35 Serug
	Nahor
	Terah
Abraham	**Abraham**
Mat 1:2 Abraham begot Isaac	Isaac
Isaac begot Jacob	Luke 3:34 Jacob
Jacob begot Judah	Judah

Matthew 1:2-16	Luke (3:23-38)
Mat 1:3 Judah begot Perez	Perez
Perez begot Hezron	Hezron
Hezron begot Ram	Ram
Mat 1:4 Ram begot Amminadab	Luke 3:33 Amminadab
Amminadab begot Nahshon	Nahshon
Nahshon begot Salmon	Salmon
Mat 1:5 Salmon begot Boaz	Boaz
Boaz begot Obed	Obed
Obed begot Jesse	Luke 3:32 Jesse
Mat 1:6 Jesse begot **David**	**David**
David the king begot *Solomon* (of Bathsheba)	*Nathan* (of Bathsheba)
Mat 1:7 *Rehoboam*	*Mattathah*
Rehoboam begot Abijah	Menan
Asa	Melea
Mat 1:8 Jehoshaphat	Eliakim
Joram	Jonan
Uzziah	Joseph
Mat 1:9 Jotham	Judah
Ahaz	Simeon
Hezekiah	Luke 3:30 Levi
Mat 1:10 Manasseh	Matthat
Amon	Jorim
Josiah	Eliezer
Mat 1:11 Jeconiah about the time they were carried away to **Babylon**	Jose
Mat 1:12 And after they were brought to **Babylon**, Jeconiah begot Shealtiel	Luke 3:29 Er
Zerubbabel	Elmodan
Mat 1:13 *Abiud*	Cosam
Eliakim	Addi
Eliakim begot Azor	Melchi
Mat 1:14 Azor begot Zadok	Luke 3:28 Neri
Zadok begot Achim	Shealtiel

Matthew 1:2-16	*Luke (3:23-38)*
Achim begot Eliud	**Zerubbabel**
Mat 1:15 Eliud begot Eleazar	*Rhesa*
Eleazar begot Matthan	Joannas
Matthan begot Jacob	Luke 3:27 Judah
Mat 1:16 **Jacob** begot Joseph the husband of Mary	Joseph
of whom was born Jesus who is called Christ.	Semei
	Mattahiah
	Maath
	Luke 3:26 Naggai
	Esli
	Nahum
	Amos
	Mattathiah
	Luke 3:25 Joseph
	Janna
	Melchi
	Levi
	Matthat
	Luke 3:24 **Heli**
	Joseph
	Luke 3:23 Jesus [was supposed] the son of Joseph

II. GENERAL RESPONSE

1. Adam Clarke's *Commentary on the Bible*

Adam Clarke's *Commentary on the Bible* addresses this issue as follows:

Matthew, in descending from Abraham to Joseph, the spouse of the blessed virgin, speaks of Sons properly such, by way of natural generation: Abraham begat Isaac, and Isaac begat Jacob, etc. But Luke, in ascending from the Savior of the world to God himself, speaks of sons either properly or improperly such: on this account he uses an indeterminate mode of expression, which may be applied to sons either *putatively* or *really* such. And Jesus himself began to be about thirty years of age, being, as was Supposed the son of Joseph - of Heli - of Matthat, etc. This receives considerable support from Raphelius's method of reading the original ων (ὡς ενομιζετο υιος Ιωσηφ) του Ἡλι, being (when reputed the son of Joseph) the son of Heli, etc. That St. Luke does not always speak of sons properly such, is evident from the first and last person which he names: Jesus Christ was only the supposed son of Joseph, because Joseph was the husband of his mother Mary: and Adam, who is said to be the son of God, was such only by creation. After this observation it is next necessary to consider, that, in the genealogy described by St. Luke, there are two sons improperly such: i.e. two sons-in-law, instead of two sons. As the Hebrews never permitted women to enter into their genealogical tables, whenever a family happened to end with a daughter, instead of naming her in the genealogy, they inserted her husband, as the son of him who was, in reality, but his father-in-law. This import, bishop Pearce has fully shown, νομιζεσθαι bears, in a variety of places - Jesus was considered according to law, or allowed custom, to be the son of Joseph, as he was of Heli. The two sons-in-law who are to be noticed in this genealogy are Joseph the son-in-law of Heli, whose own father was Jacob, Mat_1:16; and Salathiel, the son-in-law of Neri, whose own father was Jechonias: 1Ch_3:17, and Mat_1:12. This remark alone is sufficient to remove every difficulty. Thus it appears that Joseph, son of Jacob, according to St. Matthew, was son-in-law of Heli, according to St. Luke. And Salathiel, son of Jechonias, according to the former, was son-in-law of Neri, according to the latter. Mary therefore appears to have been the daughter of Heli; so called by abbreviation for Heliachim, which is the same in Hebrew with Joachim. Joseph, son of Jacob, and Mary; daughter of Heli, were of the same family: both came from Zerubbabel; Joseph from Abiud, his eldest son, Mat_1:13, and Mary by Rhesa, the youngest. See Luk_3:27. Salathiel and Zorobabel, from whom St. Matthew and St. Luke cause Christ to proceed, were themselves descended from Solomon in a direct line: and though St. Luke says that Salathiel was son of Neri, who was descended from Nathan, Solomon's eldest brother, 1Ch_3:5, this is only to be understood of his having espoused Nathan's daughter, and that Neri dying, probably, without male issues the two branches of the family of David, that of Nathan and that of Solomon, were both united in the person of Zerubbabel, by the marriage of Salathiel, chief of the regal family of Solomon, with the daughter of Neri, chief and heretrix of the family of Nathan. Thus it appears that Jesus, son of Mary, reunited in himself all the blood, privileges, and rights of the whole family of David; in consequence of which he is emphatically called, The son of David. It is worthy of being remarked that St. Matthew, who wrote principally for the Jews, extends his genealogy to Abraham through whom the promise of the Messiah was given to the Jews; but St. Luke, who wrote his history for the instruction of the Gentiles, extends his genealogy to Adam, to whom the promise of the Redeemer was given in behalf of himself and of all his posterity. See the notes on Mat 1:1, etc.

2. Support for Clarke's Arguments

While Luke recounts the names of the putative ascendants of Jesus, Matthew recounts the names of the biological descendants of Abraham.

a. Matthew Uses the Term "Begat" (γεννάω / gennáō)

This is made clear by the fact that Matthew uses the Greek "begat" (εγεννησεν/G1080) throughout the generational chain:

2 αβρααμG11 N-PRI εγεννησενG1080 V-AAI-3S τονG3588 T-ASM ισαακG2464 N-PRI ισαακG2464 N-PRI δεG1161 CONJ εγεννησενG1080 V-AAI-3S τονG3588 T-ASM ιακωβG2384 N-PRI ιακωβG2384 N-PRI δεG1161 CONJ εγεννησενG1080 V-AAI-3S τονG3588 T-ASM ιουδανG2455 N-ASM καιG2532 CONJ τουςG3588 T-APM αδελφουςG80 N-APM αυτουG846 P-GSM

Strong's Definitions defines the term γεννάω (gennáō) as "procreate (properly, of the father, but by extension of the mother); figuratively, to regenerate:—bear, beget, be born, bring forth, conceive, be delivered of, gender, make, spring."

b. Luke Recounts the Putative and Actual Ascendants of Jesus, Often without Actually Stating the Word "Son"

Luke, on the other hand, does not use the term "begat." Rather, he references a chain of descendants by referring to "sons," but at times he omits the word "son" or references a "supposed" son, making it clear that his is not intended as a genealogical list. Rather, Luke recounts the names of both putative and actual ascendants of Jesus. The original manuscripts literally read as follows (Luke 3:23-24):

> Jesus "was supposed [*the*] son of Joseph, [*the son*] of Heli, the son of Matthat, [*the son*] of Levi, [*the son*] of Melchi

The items in brackets and italics are not found in the original text and were added by translators for the sake of clarity in the translation:

> And^{G2532} Jesus^{G2424} himself^{G846} began^{G756} to be^{G2258} about^{G5616} thirty years of age,^{G5144} ^{G2094} being^{G5607} (as^{G5613} was supposed)^{G3543} the^{G3588} son^{G5207} of Joseph,^{G2501} which was [*the son*] of Heli,^{G2242}
>
> και^{G2532} CONJ αυτος^{G846} P-NSM ην^{G1510} V-IAI-3S ο^{G3588} T-NSM ιησους^{G2424} N-NSM ωσει^{G5616} ADV ετων^{G2094} N-GPN τριακοντα^{G5144} A-NUI αρχομενος^{G756} V-PMP-NSM ων^{G1510} V-PAP-NSM ως^{G5613} ADV ενομιζετο^{G3543} V-IPI-3S υιος^{G5207} N-NSM ιωσηφ^{G2501} N-PRI του^{G3588} T-GSM ηλι^{G2242} N-PRI

The original of Matthew 1:2-16, in contrast, quite literally lists generations. The English, "A begat B; and B begat C; and C begat D," etc., is present in the original Greek. For example:

> Mat 1:2 Abraham^{G11} begat^{G1080} Isaac;^{G2464} and^{G1161} Isaac^{G2464} begat^{G1080} Jacob;^{G2384} and^{G1161} Jacob^{G2384} begat^{G1080} Judas^{G2455} and^{G2532} his^{G846} brethren;^{G80}
>
> Mat 1:2 αβρααμ^{G11} N-PRI εγεννησεν^{G1080} V-AAI-3S τον^{G3588} T-ASM ισαακ^{G2464} N-PRI ισαακ^{G2464} N-PRI δε^{G1161} CONJ εγεννησεν^{G1080} V-AAI-3S

τονG3588 T-ASM ιακωβG2384 N-PRI ιακωβG2384 N-PRI δεG1161 CONJ εγεννησενG1080 V-AAI-3S τονG3588 T-ASM ιουδανG2455 N-ASM καιG2532 CONJ τουςG3588 T-APM αδελφουςG80 N-APM αυτουG846 P-GSM

c. Luke's Account Includes Two Sons-In-Law

Clarke notes that "[a]s the Hebrews never permitted women to enter into their genealogical tables, whenever a family happened to end with a daughter, instead of naming her in the genealogy, they inserted her husband, as the son of him who was, in reality, but his father-in-law … The two sons-in-law who are to be noticed in this genealogy are *Joseph* the son-in-law of Heli, whose own father was Jacob, Mat 1:16; and *Salathiel* [Shealtiel], the son-in-law of Neri, whose own father was Jechonias [Jeconiah]: 1Ch 3:17, and Mat 1:12. Mary therefore appears to have been the daughter of Heli; so called by abbreviation for Heliachim, which is the same in Hebrew with Joachim."

Clarke continues: "Joseph, son of Jacob, and Mary, daughter of Heli, were of the same family: both came from Zerubbabel; Joseph from Abiud, [Zerubbabel's] eldest son, Mat 1:13, and Mary by Rhesa, the youngest [son of Zerubbabel]. See Luk 3:27."

III. RESPONSES TO INDIVIDUAL CLAIMS

1. Matthew States that Joseph's Father Was Jacob, but Luke States It Was Heli

Dr. Philips notes that "in Matthew, the author records Jesus' paternal grandfather as being Jacob, while in Luke he is Heli" (p. 27). Matthew states that Jacob begot Joseph (Mat 1:16), but Luke does not in fact state that Heli was Luke's father. Luke literally states that Jesus was "(as was supposed) the son of Joseph, of Heli" (Luke 3:23-24). The Greek does not include the words "son of" before Heli. The addition of the words was inserted by translators, since the literal Greek "of Heli" does not translate properly in English grammar. The Greek could have meant, and very likely did mean, that Joseph was the son-in-law of Heli, who was Mary's father Joachim, which is the same in Hebrew as Heliachim, which is abbreviated in Luke as "Heli." Therefore, there is no contradiction if reviewing the original Greek of Luke 3:23, which does not state that Joseph was the son of Heli.

2. If Matthew Recounts Joseph's Genealogy and Luke Recounts Mary's, There Cannot Be Differences After David

Dr. Philip's writes that if "one were to accept the suggestion of some that one of the lists is actually the genealogy of Mary, it could not possibly account for any differences after their common ancestor David" (p. 27). If Dr. Philips means that the ascendants of David would need to be same in both Matthew and Luke, then there is no issue here, since Matthew and Luke both recount the ascendants of David as Jesse, son of Obed, son of Boaz, son of Salmon, son of Nahshon, son of Amminadab, son of Ram, son of Hezron, son of Perez, son of Judah, son of Jacob, son of Isaac, son of Abraham.

If, however, Dr. Philips means that the two lists would need to have the same descendants after David, this is not necessarily the case. Joseph could have very well been a descendent of David's son Solomon, while Mary was a descendent of David's son Nathan.

CHAPTER 12. GOD GIVES "GOOD THINGS" OR THE "HOLY SPIRIT" TO THOSE WHO ASK

I. CONTRADICTORY VERSES

"If a son asks for bread from any father among you, will he give him a stone? Or if he asks for a fish, will he give him a serpent instead of a fish? Or if he asks for an egg, will he offer him a scorpion? If you then, being evil, know how to give good gifts to your children, how much more will your heavenly Father give the Holy Spirit to those who ask Him!"" (Luke 11:11-13).

"Or what man is there among you who, if his son asks for bread, will give him a stone? Or if he asks for a fish, will he give him a serpent? If you then, being evil, know how to give good gifts to your children, how much more will your Father who is in heaven give good things to those who ask Him!" (Mat 7:9).

II. EXPLANATION

Luke 11 is presented within the context of Jesus' general teaching. Matthew 7, in contrast, is presented as part of Jesus' Matthew 5-7 Sermon on the Mount.

It is therefore possible that while preaching on the Mount, Jesus said that God gives "good things" to those who ask, but that in a separate sermon within a different context, Jesus said that God gives the Holy Spirit to those who ask.

It is thus possible that Jesus preached similar themes in different places.

CHAPTER 13. GOD PUNISHES CHILDREN FOR THEIR PARENTS' SIN, BUT EACH PERSON DIES FOR HIS OWN SIN

I. GOD PUNISHES CHILDREN FOR THEIR PARENTS' SIN TO THE THIRD AND FOURTH GENERATION

"I, the Lord your God, am a jealous God, visiting the iniquity of the fathers upon the children to the third and fourth generations of those who hate Me" (Deu 5:9) (NKJV).

The Bible in Basic English translates this as, "I, the Lord your God, am a God who will not give his honour to another; and I will send punishment on the children for the wrongdoing of their fathers, to the third and fourth generation of my haters" (Deu 5:9) (BBE).

The International Standard Version translates this as, I "am a jealous God, punishing the children for the iniquity of their parents, to the third and fourth generations of those who hate me" (Deu 5:9) (ISV).

II. YET EACH PERSON DIES (DEATH) FOR HIS OWN SIN

"Fathers shall not be put to death for their children, nor shall children be put to death for their fathers; a person shall be put to death for his own sin" (Deu 24:16).

"But every one shall die for his own iniquity; every man who eats the sour grapes, his teeth shall be set on edge" (Jer 31:30).

"The soul who sins shall die" (Eze 18:4) ... "The soul who sins shall die. The son shall not bear the guilt of the father, nor the father bear the guilt of the son. The righteousness of the righteous shall be upon himself, and the wickedness of the wicked shall be upon himself" (Eze 18:20).

III. DO THE PASSAGES CONTRADICT EACH OTHER?

There is an apparent contradiction between the passages.

On the one hand, God punishes the children for the iniquity of their parents, to the third and fourth generations (Deu 5:9); on the other hand, children shall not be put to death for their fathers' sin (Deu 24:16).

IV. RESOLUTION 1: PUNISHMENT OF CHILDREN IS ALLOWED, BUT NOT DEATH

One possible resolution of this apparent contradiction is to conclude that God may punish children for their parents' sins, but He may not put them to death. However, this explanation is inadequate because children are frequently put to death in the Bible for their parents' sin. For example:

- All of the children of the world were put to death in the great flood that was on the earth for 40 days (Gen 7:17).
- God sent fire and brimstone from heaven (Gen 19:24) and overthrew Sodom and Gomorrah and all of their inhabitants (Gen 19:25), including of course children.
- God commanded Saul to kill all of the Amelkites, including the children and infants (1Sa 15:1-3).

One may attempt to reconcile this contradiction by arguing that in the above passages, children are being put to death not for their parents' sins but for their own sins. In other words, children were also implicated in sin. The problem with this explanation however is that God's destruction of entire cities (Sodom and Gomorrah), peoples (the Amelkites) or even the world (the great flood) includes the destruction of all children, including those not yet having reach the age of accountability. This is made clear in God's commandment to kill all of the Amelkites, including the infants (1Sa 15:1-3). An infant does not yet know God's law and therefore cannot sin against it.

Clearly, then, God can put innocent infants to death for the sins of their parents. We must therefore find another possible explanation to reconcile this reality with Deuteronomy 24:16 (stating that children shall not be put to death for their fathers' sins).

V. RESOLUTION 2: CHILDREN'S PUNISHMENT COMES ABOUT AS A NATURAL CONSEQUENCE OF THEIR FATHER'S SIN

1. Overview

A second possible explanation for the seeming contradiction requires looking to the punishment of children not as a consequence of God's actions as an active agent, but rather, as a natural consequence of the chain of cause and effect that results when one sins. One should see the punishment of children not as a result of God's decision to punish them for their father's sin, but rather, as ripples that result from the "pebble" that drops into a pond—*i.e.*, when a father sins.

2. Objection

While this explanation has some validity, it does not deal directly with the matter at hand. It is true that through a father's sin, his children face natural consequences. Just as through our father Adam's sin, we all now face sickness, disease and death, so too do the children of any father face the consequences of his sin. For example, an alcoholic father who beats his wife may become imprisoned, causing family breakup. Children may be put into protective services, breaking up the family unit. They may be forced to live with a single mother who struggles to provide financially. Such consequences would be obviated but for the sin of the father.

However, the issue that this discussion is trying to resolve is not that of the natural consequences of sin, as passive forces that enter the world through inevitable chains of cause and effect. Rather, it is the punishment of children rendered by God as an active agent.

God says that he "visit[s] the iniquity of the fathers upon the children to the third and fourth generations of those who hate Me" (Deu 5:9) (NKJV). The International Standard Version

translates this as, I "punish ... the children for the iniquity of
their parents, to the third and fourth generations of those who
hate me" (Deu 5:9) (ISV).

There is a clear element of God's actively ushering in
punishment, visiting the iniquity of parents on their children, or
punishing children for their parents' sin. In other words, it is not
that parents are sinning and, through a natural chain of cause
and effect, the children face the consequences a passive chain of
events where God is a passive observer. Rather, it is that God is
an agent in actively punishing children (e.g., by sending down
fire and brimstone (Gen 19:24) to destroy Sodom and
Gomorrah and their inhabitants (Gen 19:25)) or otherwise by
commanding the Israelites to punish children (e.g., commanding
Saul to kill all of the Amelkites, including the children and
infants (1Sa 15:1-3)).

3. Answer to Objection

Not a sparrow falls to the ground except by God's will (Mat
10:29). Therefore, all death can be said to be traced back to
God's will. The distinction between the death of Adam's
children, naturally following as a result of Adam's sin, and the
death of David's son, as a punishment for David's sin, is an
artificial one. Both when God punishes a child directly and
when he allows children to die, His will is being done.

We should not create any artificial distinction between
natural death and deaths where God appears to be an active
agent. Instances in which God ordered, for example, the
children of the Amalekites to be destroyed should not be
deemed any more a consequence of God as an active agent than
the deaths of, for example, the Japanese in the 2011 Tsunami or
the deaths of Americans and Iraqis in the 2003 invasion in Iraq
should be attributed to God as an active agent. In all of these
cases, death results from human sin, and this death, at least in an
indirect sense, according to God's will. Not a sparrow falls to
the ground apart from God's will (Mat 10:29). God is sovereign
and omnipotent; He could have created a world where there was
no possibility for sin or death, but he instead created a world in

which man's sin, rebellion and disobedience would result in death. God has the power to spare any man from death or to allow death to take any man. In at least an indirect sense, then, all death in the Bible is according to God's will, or permission, yet in Deuteronomy 24:16, God limits the ability of the Israelis to apply punishments by allowing only the sinner, not his father or child, to be put to death for his sin.

Therefore, we can view Deuteronomy 24:16 as a judicial law forbidding the punishment of children for their parents' sins and Deuteronomy 5:9 as a natural law discussing the consequences of sin reaching down to later generations. The death of children for their parents' sins throughout the Bible is not a result of the application of the Deuteronomical judicial law, but rather, it is a result of the natural law. Death came to all the world through the flood (Gen 7:17) and to all of the inhabitants of Sodom and Gomorrah (Gen 19:25) because death is the natural consequence of sin, not because the Israelites violated God's law about not putting to death a child for his father's sin.

4. Response to the Answer to the Objection

To not view God as an active agent of the punishment of children for their parents' sins in Deuteronomy contradicts the clear language of the text, which presents punishment not as an indirect consequence through natural laws but rather, as a result of God's hand as active agent and punisher:

> The International Standard Version translates this as, I "am a jealous God, punishing the children for the iniquity of their parents, to the third and fourth generations of those who hate me" (Deu 5:9) (ISV).

VI. RESOLUTION 3: DEUTERONOMY 24:16 IS PART OF THE LAW GIVEN TO THE ISRAELITES TO BIND THE ISRAELITES, BUT GOD HAD THE RIGHT TO ENACT INTERGENERATIONAL VICARIOUS PUNISHMENT

1. The More Appropriate Explanation

The more appropriate explanation for the seeming
contradiction is that while Deuteronomy 24:16 prohibits the
Israelites from undertaking intergenerational vicarious
punishment, it does not prohibit God. Deuteronomy 24:16
applies to men, but it does not limit God in His dealings with
men.

Deuteronomy 5:9 deals with how God punishes sin. He
punishes sin to the third and fourth generation of those that hate
Him.

Deuteronomy 24:16, in contrast, deals with the law given to
the Israelites to govern their acts, sins and consequences of sin.
He enumerates a series of laws and consequences of breaching
the laws. For example, if a man kidnaps an Israeli and mistreats
or sells him, then the kidnapper is to die (Deu 24:7).
Deuteronomy 24:16 deals with the consequences to be imposed
on sinners. God makes it clear that the death penalty was to be
applied to sinners, not to their children or parents.

The prohibition on the Israelites from punishing children for
their father's sins does not prohibit God from punishing sin by
any means, including by killing the children of the sinner.

On this basis, we can see that in the Old Testament, one's
sins frequently lead to the death of his children:

- All of the children of the world were put to death in the
  great flood that was on the earth for 40 days (Gen 7:17).
- God sent fire and brimstone from heaven (Gen 19:24)
  and overthrew Sodom and Gomorrah and all of their
  inhabitants (Gen 19:25). It is reasonable to assume that
  children and infants living in Sodom and Gomorrah
  were also put to death.
- God commanded Saul to kill all of the Amelkites,
  including the children and infants (1Sa 15:1-3).
- Nathan told King David that because of David's sin, his
  child would die: "However, because by this deed you
  have given great occasion to the enemies of the Lord to
  blaspheme, the child also who is born to you shall surely
  die" (2Sa 12:14). The Lord struck David's child with an

illness (2Sa 12:15) and the child died after seven days (2Sa 12:18).

It is important to note however that in all of these instances, it is God who is doing the punishing. The Israelites, in contrast, were not permitted to punish children for their parents' sins.

2. How the Case of Achan (Jos 7) Fits into Resolution 3

a. The Account of Achan is Troublesome under Resolution 2's Paradigm

In the book of Joshua, we read that about three thousand men were sent to Ai, but they were routed (Jos 7:3-4) and about thirty-six of them were killed (Jos 7:5). Joshua tore his clothes and inquired of the Lord (Jos 7:6-7), who revealed that Israel had sinned: They deceived and took some of the devoted things (Jos 7:11). God commanded Joshua to bring the tribes. The tribe that the Lord took was to come forward clan by clan; the clan that the Lord took was to come forward family by family; the family that the Lord took was to come household by household and then man by man (Jos 7:14) and the one taken with the devoted thing was to be burned with fire along with all that he has (Jos 7:15).

The next morning, Achan the son of Carmi was taken (Jos 7:16-18) and confessed that he had taken the spoils of a Babylonian garment, two hundred shekels of silver and a wedge of gold, all hidden in his tent (Jos 7:21).

Then Joshua and all of Israel took Achan and his children and possessions (Jos 7:24) and stoned him and burned them with fire after they had stoned them (Jos 7:25).

b. Why Achan's Children Were Put to Death

If God commanded that children shall not be put to death for their fathers, but only for their own sin (Deu 24:16), then why were Achan's children put to death? There are several possible explanations:

a. *Only Achan was put to death.*

The rendering of Joshua 7:25-26 is not entirely clear, and there are discrepancies among some translations. What is clear is that Achan was stoned and burned with fire, his family was burned with fire and Achan was buried in a heap of rocks. However, what is not clear is whether Achan's family was actually killed in the fire.

The NIV, NKJV and ASV state only that Achan was buried and the ISV states only that Achan was stoned to death. This leaves open the possibility that although Achan's family was burned, they were not actually killed or buried.

However, this explanation is problematic in that it is highly unlikely that the Israelites would stone or burn someone without killing him. Stoning and burning were punishments unto death.

b.   *The Israelites violated Deuteronomy 24:16 by putting the children to death.*

This explanation is problematic because it seems that God commanded that the children also be destroyed by fire. In Joshua 7:15, He commands that "he who is taken with the accursed thing shall be burned with fire, he and all that he has," with "all that he has" implying his family as well.

c.   *The children participated in the father's sin and were therefore also culpable.*

This explanation has some biblical support. In revealing to Joshua Israel's sin, God's language implicates more than one person. He says, "they have also transgressed My covenant"; "they have even taken some of the accursed things, and have both stolen and deceived" and "they have also put it among their own stuff" (Jos 7:11).

With the implication being that more than one person was involved in the sin, God commanded that "he who is taken with the accursed thing shall be burned with fire, he and all that he has," which implies that the person's family was implicated in the sin (Jos 7:15).

Because the devoted things were later found to be in Achan's tent, it is reasonable to conclude that his family, which would have also stayed in the tent, at least had knowledge of, if not complicity in, the sin.

Yet even if Achan's family was not implicated in the sin, God's commandment that Achan's children be killed is not necessarily contrary to Deuteronomy 24:16 (children are not to be put to death for their fathers' sins). As explained above, this was a law given to the Israelites, but God was permitted, as he had done here (Jos 7:15), to punish the children of sinners who hate Him, in accordance with Deuteronomy 5:9. God is not bound by the law given to the Israelites.

CHAPTER 14. HAS ANYONE SEEN GOD?

I. PROBLEM 1: JOHN WROTE THAT NO ONE HAS SEEN GOD, BUT THERE ARE MULTIPLE ACCOUNTS OF SEEING GOD

1. Overview

On the one hand, John wrote:

John 1:18 No one has seen God at any time. The only begotten Son, who is in the bosom of the Father, He has declared Him.

2. Accounts of Those Who Saw God

However, there are many accounts of individuals who saw God:

- Abraham: The "Lord" appeared before Abraham and promised he would have a son.
- Jacob: Jacob wrestled with a Man and stated, "I have seen God face to face" (Gen 32:30).
- Moses, Aaron, Nadab, Abihu and Seventy Elders of Israel: They saw God (Exo 24:9-10);
- King Nebuchadnezzar: God appeared before King Nebuchadnezzar in the furnace with Shadrach, Meshach and Abed-Nego.
- Jesus: Jesus was seen, and he was ostensibly God (and the Son of God).

a. The "Lord" Appeared to Abraham as Three Men and Promised Abraham would have a Son (Gen 18:1-6)

The "Lord" appeared to Abraham and promised that he would have a son in his old age:

Gen 18:1 Then the Lord appeared to him by the terebinth trees of Mamre, as he was sitting in the tent door in the heat of the day.

Gen 18:2 So he lifted his eyes and looked, and behold, three men were standing by him; and when he saw them, he ran from the tent door to meet them, and bowed himself to the ground,

Gen 18:3 and said, "My Lord, if I have now found favor in Your sight, do not pass on by Your servant.

Gen 18:4 Please let a little water be brought, and wash your feet, and rest yourselves under the tree.

Gen 18:5 And I will bring a morsel of bread, that you may refresh your hearts. After that you may pass by, inasmuch as you have come to your servant." They said, "Do as you have said."

Gen 18:6 So Abraham hurried into the tent to Sarah and said, "Quickly, make ready three measures of fine meal; knead it and make cakes."

b.   Jacob Wrestled with God and Saw "God Face to Face" (Gen 32:24-30)

Jacob reported not only that he saw God, but that he saw God "face to face," yet lived (Gen 32:30) after wrestling with a "Man" (Gen 32:24) whom Jacob surmised was God:

Gen 32:24 Then Jacob was left alone; and a Man wrestled with him until the breaking of day.

Gen 32:25 Now when He saw that He did not prevail against him, He touched the socket of his hip; and the socket of Jacob's hip was out of joint as He wrestled with him.

Gen 32:26 And He said, "Let Me go, for the day breaks." But he said, "I will not let You go unless You bless me!"

Gen 32:27 So He said to him, "What is your name?" He said, "Jacob."

Gen 32:28 And He said, "Your name shall no longer be called Jacob, but Israel; for you have struggled with God and with men, and have prevailed."

Gen 32:29 Then Jacob asked, saying, "Tell me Your name, I pray." And He said, "Why is it that you ask about My name?" And He blessed him there.

Gen 32:30 So Jacob called the name of the place Peniel: "For I have seen God face to face, and my life is preserved."

Genesis 32:24 refers to the person as a "Man," but the context implies that it is no ordinary man with whom Jacob wrestled. The person has supernatural qualities. Genesis 32:28 states that Jacob struggled "with God and with men, and [had] prevailed." Presumably, the struggle being referred to was the struggle in Genesis 32:24, where "a Man wrestled" with Jacob. If the "Man" had the qualities of "God and men," as referenced in Genesis 32:28, then the figure was likely Jesus, who was God in the form of man. The fact that Jacob, in Genesis 32:30, states, "I have seen God face to face" is further indication that the Man he wrestled with was God.

c. God Appeared to Moses as an Angel through a Burning Bush (Exo 3:2)

God appeared to Moses as an angel through a burning bush (Exo 3:2):

Exo 3:1 Now Moses was tending the flock of Jethro his father-in-law, the priest of Midian. And he led the flock to the back of the desert, and came to Horeb, the mountain of God.
Exo 3:2 And the Angel of the Lord appeared to him in a *flame of fire from the midst of a bush*. So he looked, and behold, the bush was burning with fire, but *the bush was not consumed*.
Exo 3:3 Then Moses said, "I will now turn aside and see this great sight, why the bush does not burn."
Exo 3:4 So when the Lord saw that he turned aside to look, God called to him from the midst of the bush and said, "Moses, Moses!" And he said, "Here I am."
Exo 3:5 Then He said, "Do not draw near this place. *Take your sandals off your feet, for the place where you stand is holy ground*."

d. Moses, Aaron, Nadab, Abihu and Seventy Elders of Israel Saw God (Exo 24:9-10)

Moses, Aaron, Nadab, Abihu and seventy elders of Israel saw God:

Exo 24:9 Then Moses went up, also Aaron, Nadab, and Abihu, and seventy of the elders of Israel,

Exo 24:10 and they saw the God of Israel. And there was under His feet as it were a paved work of sapphire stone, and it was like the very heavens in its clarity.

e.   The Son of God Appeared in the Furnace with Shadrach, Meshach and Abed-Nego (Dan 3:23-28)

The book of Daniel reports that after King Nebuchadnezzar cast Shadrach, Meschach and Abed-Nego into the fiery furnace, he witnessed a fourth man with them and "the form of the fourth is like the Son of God." It appears that this fourth man was Jesus.

Dan 3:23 And these three men, Shadrach, Meshach, and Abed-Nego, fell down bound into the midst of the burning fiery furnace.
Dan 3:24 Then King Nebuchadnezzar was astonished; and he rose in haste and spoke, saying to his counselors, "Did we not cast three men bound into the midst of the fire?" They answered and said to the king, "True, O king."
Dan 3:25 "Look!" he answered, "I see four men loose, walking in the midst of the fire; and they are not hurt, and the *form of the fourth is like the Son of God*."
Dan 3:26 Then Nebuchadnezzar went near the mouth of the burning fiery furnace and spoke, saying, "Shadrach, Meshach, and Abed-Nego, servants of the Most High God, come out, and come here." Then Shadrach, Meshach, and Abed-Nego came from the midst of the fire.
Dan 3:27 And the satraps, administrators, governors, and the king's counselors gathered together, and they saw these men on whose bodies the fire had no power; the hair of their head was not singed nor were their garments affected, and the smell of fire was not on them.
Dan 3:28 Nebuchadnezzar spoke, saying, "Blessed be the God of Shadrach, Meshach, and Abed-Nego, who sent His Angel and delivered His servants who trusted in Him, and they have frustrated the king's word, and yielded their bodies, that they should not serve nor worship any god except their own God!

3.   Accounts of Those Who Had Visions of God

In addition, several Scriptures state that God was seen in visions.

a. Micaiah's Vision of the Lord Putting a Lying Spirit in the
    Mouth of Ahab's Prophets (2Ch 18:18-22)

Elijah's disciple Micaiah reported a vision where he saw the
Lord sitting on His throne and sending a lying spirit to the
mouth of Ahab's prophets (2Ch 18:18-22):

> 2Ch 18:18 Then Micaiah said, "Therefore hear the word of
> the Lord: I saw the Lord *sitting on His throne*, and all the host
> of heaven standing on His right hand and His left.
> 2Ch 18:19 And the Lord said, 'Who will persuade Ahab king
> of Israel to go up, that he may fall at Ramoth Gilead?' So one
> spoke in this manner, and another spoke in that manner.
> 2Ch 18:20 Then a spirit came forward and stood before the
> Lord, and said, 'I will persuade him.' The Lord said to him, 'In
> what way?'
> 2Ch 18:21 So he said, 'I will go out and be a lying spirit in the
> mouth of all his prophets.' And the Lord said, 'You shall
> persuade him and also prevail; go out and do so.'
> 2Ch 18:22 Therefore look! The Lord has put a lying spirit in
> the mouth of these prophets of yours, and the Lord has
> declared disaster against you."

b. Isaiah's Vision of God Sitting on a Throne (Isa 6:1-4)

Isaiah saw a vision of God sitting on a throne, high and
lifted up (Isa 6:1-4):

> Isa 6:1 In the year that King Uzziah died, I saw the Lord
> *sitting on a throne*, high and lifted up, and the train of His
> robe filled the temple.
> Isa 6:2 Above it stood seraphim; each one had six wings: with
> two he covered his face, with two he covered his feet, and
> with two he flew.
> Isa 6:3 And one cried to another and said: "Holy, holy, holy is
> the Lord of hosts; The whole earth is full of His glory!"
> Isa 6:4 And the posts of the door were shaken by the voice of
> him who cried out, and the house was filled with smoke.

c. Daniel's Vision of the "Ancient of Days" (Dan 7:9)

Daniel writes of a vision of the "Ancient of Days" who was
enthroned and clothed in garment as white as snow:

Dan 7:9 "I watched till thrones were put in place, And the Ancient of Days was seated; His *garment was white as snow*, And the hair of His head was like pure wool. His throne was a fiery flame, Its wheels a burning fire;

Dan 7:10 A fiery stream issued And came forth from before Him. A thousand thousands ministered to Him; Ten thousand times ten thousand stood before Him. The court was seated, And the books were opened.

Dan 7:11 "I watched then because of the sound of the pompous words which the horn was speaking; I watched till the beast was slain, and its body destroyed and given to the burning flame.

Dan 7:12 As for the rest of the beasts, they had their dominion taken away, yet their lives were prolonged for a season and a time.

Dan 7:13 "I was watching in the night visions, And behold, One like the Son of Man, Coming with the clouds of heaven! He came to the Ancient of Days, And they brought Him near before Him.

Dan 7:14 Then to Him was given dominion and glory and a kingdom, That all peoples, nations, and languages should serve Him. His dominion is an everlasting dominion, Which shall not pass away, And His kingdom the one Which shall not be destroyed.

d.   Amos' Vision of God and the Prophecy of Syria (Amos 1:1-5)

Amos writes of a vision in which God speaks to him of the captivity of the Syrians (Amos 1:1-5):

Amos 1:1 The words of Amos, who was among the sheepbreeders of Tekoa, which he saw concerning Israel in the days of Uzziah king of Judah, and in the days of Jeroboam the son of Joash, king of Israel, two years before the earthquake.

Amos 1:2 And he said: "The Lord roars from Zion, And utters His voice from Jerusalem; The pastures of the shepherds mourn, And the top of Carmel withers."

Amos 1:3 Thus says the Lord: "For three transgressions of Damascus, and for four, I will not turn away its punishment, Because they have threshed Gilead with implements of iron.

Amos 1:4 But I will send a fire into the house of Hazael, Which shall devour the palaces of Ben-Hadad.

Amos 1:5 I will also break the gate bar of Damascus, And cut off the inhabitant from the Valley of Aven, And the one who holds the scepter from Beth Eden. The people of Syria shall go captive to Kir," Says the Lord.

e. John's Vision of God (Rev 1:9-18)

John, while on the island of Patmos, writes of a vision of "One like the Son of Man, clothed with a white garment down to the feet and girded about the chest with a golden band" while John was in the Spirit (Rev 1:9-18):

Rev 1:9 I, John, both your brother and companion in the tribulation and kingdom and patience of Jesus Christ, was on the island that is called Patmos for the word of God and for the testimony of Jesus Christ.

Rev 1:10 I was in the Spirit on the Lord's Day, and I heard behind me a loud voice, as of a trumpet,

Rev 1:11 saying, "I am the Alpha and the Omega, the First and the Last," and, "What you see, write in a book and send it to the seven churches which are in Asia: to Ephesus, to Smyrna, to Pergamos, to Thyatira, to Sardis, to Philadelphia, and to Laodicea."

Rev 1:12 Then I turned to see the voice that spoke with me. And having turned I saw *seven golden lampstands*,

Rev 1:13 and in the midst of the seven lampstands *One like the Son of Man, clothed with a garment down to the feet and girded about the chest with a golden band*.

Rev 1:14 *His head and hair were white like wool, as white as snow, and His eyes like a flame of fire*;

Rev 1:15 His feet were like fine brass, as if refined in a furnace, and His voice as the sound of many waters;

Rev 1:16 He had in His right hand seven stars, out of His mouth went a sharp two-edged sword, and His countenance was like the sun shining in its strength.

Rev 1:17 And when I saw Him, I fell at His feet as dead. But He laid His right hand on me, saying to me, "Do not be afraid; I am the First and the Last.

Rev 1:18 I am He who lives, and was dead, and behold, I am alive forevermore. Amen. And I have the keys of Hades and of Death.

4. Response

a. Explanation 1: John Had Not Read the Old Testament and Was Mistaken

a. Overview

One possibility is that John, a fisherman who was regarded as "uneducated and untrained" by the rulers, elders, scribes and high priest (Acts 4:5-13), simply had not read the Old Testament accounts of Moses, Aaron, Abraham, Jacob and others seeing God. Therefore, he was mistaken when he reported that "No one has seen God" (John 1:18).

b. Problem with Proposed Explanation

There are multiple problems with this explanation. First, it presumes that John's Gospel was not the divinely inspired word of God. Certainly, if irreconcilable contradictions appear within John or between John and other texts of the Bible, this view could potentially hold ground. However, before coming to such a conclusion, we must explore whether there are credible explanations that reconcile John 1:18 with earlier accounts of God being seen. As discussed below, such explanations exist.

Second, just because the rulers, elders, scribes and high priest perceive something to be so does not mean it is so. These are the same men that denied Jesus' divinity and plotted to have Him crucified. They failed to recognize Jesus as God's only begotten Son. Just as they erred in their perception of Jesus, they may have erred in their perception of John, who may have in fact been educated and trained. While John may have been a fisherman, it does not necessarily follow that he was uneducated.

Regardless of whether John was educated and trained, he was likely well-versed in the Scriptures. Hebrew children like John were traditionally required to memorize the first five books of Torah before they were twelve years old. They were also required to discuss these texts and write them. It is unlikely that John not exempt from this requirement. The theological richness of the Gospel of John indicates that John was well-versed in the Old Testament. Throughout his Gospel, John quotes from the Old Testament (see, e.g., John 1:23, taken from Isaiah). Moreover, even if John were not specifically educated and trained in the Bible, it is highly unlikely that as a Jew, he would be unaware of the stories of the Old Testament whereby the great prophets, including Moses, and the patriarchs, including Abraham and Jacob (Israel), were said to have seen God. Finally, the depth of writing and spiritual insight contained in John's book of Revelation undermines the characterization of John as "uneducated and untrained" by the rulers, elders, scribes and the high priest.

b. Explanation 2: John Meant "No One Has Seen God" in All His Glory

a. Overview

i. The Manifestations of God to Moses, Jacob, Abraham and Others Were Not Total

When John wrote "no one has seen God" (John 1:18), he was conveying an idea that was not in conflict with the accounts of Moses, Aaron, Jacob, Abraham and other accounts of sightings of God in the Old Testament. Rather, he meant that no person had ever seen God in his totality (*i.e.*, in all of His glory). The accounts we find in the Old Testament sightings of God are partial views of God. When God was revealed to Moses and to others, he hid his face (*e.g.*, Exo 33:23) or took on a form other than his full, true essence:

-   He appeared to Moses as an angel through a burning bush (Exo 3:2);
-   He appeared to Moses, Aaron, Nadab, Abihu and seventy elders (Exo 24:9-10);
-   He appeared to Jacob as a "man" who wrestled him (Gen 32:24-30);
-   He appeared to Abraham as "three men" (Gen 18:1-6);
-   He appeared to King Nebuchadnezzar as "the Son of God" in the fiery furnace (Dan 3:23-28).

All of these appearances to man were not total and were not in all of God's glory. While God has manifested himself in manifold ways throughout history, no one has seen God revealed in all His glory. If God were to totally reveal Himself to sinful humans, they would be consumed. Therefore, God transforms and appears in ways that can be seen, but that are not manifestations of God in his full glory. We can "see" him, but not with all of His glory and holiness exhibited. Moreover, God, as an omnipresent being, cannot be fully perceived with human eyes. Only portions of God that He chooses to manifest may be seen by man.

In addition, the visions of God recounted by Micaiah, Isaiah, Daniel, Amos and John (in Revelation) are clearly visions and not physical encounters with God. In their visions, the prophets see God, generally in the form of a man. They recount him sitting on a throne (2Ch 18:18, Isa 6:1) and clothed in a white garment (Dan 7:9; Rev 1:14). From their context, these are clearly spiritual visions of God rather than physical sightings of God. Therefore, they do not contradict John 1:18 ("No one has seen God at any time").

ii. No One Can See God Because He Is an Invisible Spirit; the Theophanies of God Were Partial Manifestations

"God is Spirit, and those who worship Him must worship in spirit and truth" (John 4:24). A spirit is invisible. It cannot be seen with the human eye. It can be seen *in the spirit* through visions, as John saw in the book of Revelation, while he "was in the Spirit on the Lord's Day" (Rev 1:10). God can choose to manifest Himself in ways that are visible to the physical eye, as he did with Abraham as three men who promised Abraham would have a Son (Gen 18:1-6); with Jacob as a "man" who wrestled with Jacob (Gen 32:24-30); to Moses as an angel through a burning bush (Exo 3:2); and to King Nebuchadnezzar as the "Son of God" in the fiery furnace with Shadrach, Meshach and Abed-Nego (Dan 3:23-28). However, God, in all of his glory, cannot be seen to the human eye. Every vision of Him that was seen was incomplete and not total.

iii. God Was Revealed to Man as Jesus throughout the Old and New Testaments

While God can not be seen and has never been seen, he has revealed himself throughout the Old Testament and New Testament, including as the three men who visited Abraham, as "the angel of the Lord" who visited Hagar and Manoah, as the man who wrestled with Jacob, as "the angel of the Lord" who appeared to Moses in the burning bush, as "the Son of God" in the fiery furnace and as the incarnate Son of God in the New Testament. In all of these appearances, God remained unseen in His full glory, but He was declared through Jesus. As John wrote, "No one has ever seen God, but the one and only Son, who is himself God and is in closest relationship with the Father, has made him known" (John 1:18). Jesus said to Philip (John 14:9):

> Don't you know me, Philip, even after I have been among you such a long time? Anyone who has seen me has seen the Father. How can you say, 'Show us the Father'?

God therefore manifests Himself to mankind through Jesus, who appeared as a man to Abraham and Jacob, as "the angel of the Lord" to Hagar, Moses and Manoah, and as a man to the Jews and Romans in the New Testament. To appear to mankind, God must turn down the spiritual volume of His radiance and glory so that those to whom He is manifested not die.

Colossians 1:15, Colossians 2:9 and Hebrews 1:3 reveal that Jesus is the "image" of God; that in Jesus, the fullness of the Godhead dwells in bodily form; and that Jesus is the express image of God's person. Jesus, as a member of the Trinity, is the image and manifestation of God, a bodily form in which the Godhead dwells as an image of God's glory.

b. Problem with Proposed Explanation

The one text in the Old Testament that is problematic is Exodus 24:9-10, where Moses, Aaron, Nadab, Abihu and seventy elders are reported to have seen God:

> Exo 24:9 Then Moses went up, also Aaron, Nadab, and Abihu, and seventy of the elders of Israel,
> Exo 24:10 and they saw the God of Israel. And there was under His feet as it were a paved work of sapphire stone, and it was like the very heavens in its clarity.

There is nothing in this text to suggest that they only saw a physical manifestation or had a spiritual vision of God.

c. Response to Problem with Proposed Explanation

Exodus 24:9-10 state only that Moses and his companions "saw the God of Israel." It does not give the specifics of how the God of Israel was manifested. When read together with Exodus 33:20, where God stated that Moses "cannot see My face," we can presume that Moses and his companions in Exodus 24:9-10 did not see God's face. It can be concluded with a reasonable degree of certainty that the theophany of God in Exodus 24:9-10 was the same type as the many other theophanies recorded in the Scriptures, to wit:

- God's appearance to Moses as "the angel of the Lord" through a burning bush (Exo 3:2);
- Jacob's encounter with God as a man with whom Jacob wrestled (Gen 32:24-30);
- The appearance of the "Lord" to Abraham as three men who promised Abraham would have a Son (Gen 18:1-6);
- The appearance of "the Son of God" in the furnace with Shadrach, Meshach and Abed-Nego (Dan 3:23-28).

II. PROBLEM 2: GOD SAID NO ONE CAN SEE HIM AND LIVE, BUT JACOB RECOUNTED SEEING GOD "FACE TO FACE"

1. Overview

In Exodus, God said that Moses could not "see My face" and that no man shall see God and live. Presumably, He meant no man shall see God's "face" and live, since Moses saw God's back and lived:

> Exo 33:20 But He said, "You cannot see My face; for no man shall see Me, and live."
> Exo 33:21 And the Lord said, "Here is a place by Me, and you shall stand on the rock.
> Exo 33:22 So it shall be, while My glory passes by, that I will put you in the cleft of the rock, and will cover you with My hand while I pass by.

Exo 33:23 Then I will take away My hand, and you shall see My back; but My face shall not be seen."

However, Jacob reported not only that he saw God, but that he saw God "face to face," yet lived (Gen 32:30) after wrestling with a "Man" (Gen 32:24) who Jacob surmised was God:

Gen 32:24 Then Jacob was left alone; and a Man wrestled with him until the breaking of day.
Gen 32:25 Now when He saw that He did not prevail against him, He touched the socket of his hip; and the socket of Jacob's hip was out of joint as He wrestled with him.
Gen 32:26 And He said, "Let Me go, for the day breaks." But he said, "I will not let You go unless You bless me!"
Gen 32:27 So He said to him, "What is your name?" He said, "Jacob."
Gen 32:28 And He said, "Your name shall no longer be called Jacob, but Israel; for you have struggled with God and with men, and have prevailed."
Gen 32:29 Then Jacob asked, saying, "Tell me Your name, I pray." And He said, "Why is it that you ask about My name?" And He blessed him there.
Gen 32:30 So Jacob called the name of the place Peniel: "For I have seen God face to face, and my life is preserved."

Genesis 32:24 refers to the person as a "Man," but the context implies that the man was God, or a manifestation of God. Genesis 32:28 states that Jacob struggled "with God and with men, and [had] prevailed." Presumably, the struggle being referred to was the struggle in Genesis 32:24, where "a Man wrestled" with Jacob. If the "Man" had the qualities of "God and men," as referenced in Genesis 32:28, then the figure was likely Jesus, who was God in the form of man. The fact that Jacob, in Genesis 32:30, states, "I have seen God face to face" is further indication that the Man he wrestled with was God.

This leaves open a question: Why did God say to Moses that he could not see God's face and that no one could see God and live (Exo 33:20), yet Jacob wrestled with God, saw him "face to face" and lived (Gen 32:30)?

2. Response: God Revealed Himself Partially to Jacob

a. As with Moses, God Allows Partial Manifestations of Himself

When God said to Moses, "You cannot see My face; for no man shall see Me, and live" (Exo 33:20), He made clear that God could not be seen in all of His glory. However, God could allow partial manifestations of His being to be seen. Therefore, God arranged for Moses to see God's "back":

> Exo 33:21 And the Lord said, "Here is a place by Me, and you shall stand on the rock.
> Exo 33:22 So it shall be, while My glory passes by, that I will put you in the cleft of the rock, and will cover you with My hand while I pass by.
> Exo 33:23 Then I will take away My hand, and you shall see My back; but My face shall not be seen."

b. God's Manifestation to Jacob was Also Partial; Jacob May have Seen an God, but It Was Not God in His Full Power

Again, in Genesis 32:24-30, we find another partial manifestation of God, this time to Jacob. Genesis 32:24 states that Jacob encountered a "Man," but Genesis 32:28 states that Jacob struggled "with God and with men, and [had] prevailed." Presumably, then, in Genesis 32:24, the "Man" that Jacob encountered was the "God" that he struggled with in Genesis 32:28. However, it was not the full manifestation of God. The Bible teaches that God is omnipotent (Rev 19:6); that nothing is too hard for him (Jer 32:17); and that all things are possible with God (Mark 10:27). Therefore, whoever the "Man" in Genesis 32:24 was, it was not God in his full power and glory. It may have been an angel, or a partial manifestation of God in a form that Jacob could successfully wrestle against.

Alternatively, it could have been an appearance of Jesus, the incarnation of God in the form of a man. However, whether one accepts that Jesus was the "Man" who wrestled with Jacob will depend on whether one believes that Jesus is all-powerful, since the "Man" who wrestled with Jacob was unable to overpower Jacob.

Regardless of who the "Man" was, he possessed at least some supernatural power. He was able to disable Jacob simply by touching the socket of Jacob's hip:

Gen 32:25 Now when He saw that He did not prevail against him, He touched the socket of his hip; and the socket of Jacob's hip was out of joint as He wrestled with him.

As a result, Jacob "limped on his hip" (Gen 32:31).

It would be reasonable to conclude that the being that Jacob wrestled with was neither God in all of His power nor was he any ordinary man. He may have been an angel or a manifestation of God with limited power. Therefore, Jacob's statement, "I saw God face to face, and yet my life was spared" (Gen 32:30) should not be taken literally.

c. Seeing God "Face to Face" Is to Be Understood Figuratively in Jewish Thought

When Jacob said he saw God "face to face," he meant he dialogued directly with God, not that he literally saw God's face, which no man can see and live (Exo 33:20). Seeing God "face to face" in Jewish thought is distinct from seeing God's face. Seeing God face to face is to be understood as hearing God speak in plain language, as one friend speaks to another.

This is made clear in Exodus 33, where God states "no one may see me and live" (Exo 33:20), and yet, just 9 verses earlier, Exodus 33:11 reports that "The LORD would speak to Moses face to face, as one speaks to a friend" (Exo 33:11). Clearly, then, speaking to God "face to face," as in Exodus 33:11, is not the same as seeing God's face, as in Exodus 33:20. To interpret the two expressions to mean the same thing would lead to absurd consequences. It would mean that the author of Genesis, when writing that no one could see God's face in verse 33:20, would have developed a case of amnesia so severe that he forgot that just nine verses earlier, he stated that Moses saw God face to face. Therefore, speaking with God "face to face" in the sense of Genesis 33:11 must be read to mean something different from seeing God's face in Genesis 33:20, which no man may see and live.

Jacob's affirmation in Genesis 32:30 that he saw God "face to face" must be interpreted according to the meaning contained in Exodus 33:11, that is, to mean that Jacob spoke to God as Moses did, "as one speaks to a friend" (Exo 33:11). This is the meaning customarily attributed to the phrase "face to face" in Jewish through and in the Hebrew language. Chabad.org, for example, speaks of the expression "face to face" as referring to a meaning of fellowship, love and inner communication, as the word for face, *panim*, is the same as *pnimiyut*, which means "innerness"[4]:

> The Zohar explains that at the beginning of Elul we are achor el achor, meaning "back to back," and by the end of Elul we are panim el panim, "face to face." But how can it be that we are back to back? Wouldn't that imply that G-d has His back turned to us as well? How can we say such a thing, when this is the month in which—as chassidic master Rabbi Schneur Zalman of Liadi teaches us—"the King is in the field"? Is it not the month when G-d is more accessible than ever, when He is waiting for us to greet Him, when He is there for us in the "field" of our everyday lives?
>
> The fact that we are described as "back to back" and then "face to face" is an incredible lesson. Often, when we feel angry, hurt, abandoned, whatever the root of our pain may be, we turn our back. When our back is turned, we have no idea of the state of the other. And it is often easier to believe that we are not the only one with a turned back. It is easier to think the other also turned around, that the other isn't facing us at all, because if that is the case, then even if we turn around it won't help, so why bother. Why make that first move only to turn around and see the back of the other?
>
> ...
>
> Only when we turn around do we realize the truth, the inner essence, and then we are "face to face," which does not only mean that we can finally look at each other, but more so, that we can look in each other—for the root of the word for face, *panim*, is the same as *pnimiyut*, which means "innerness."
>
> ...
>
> The Jewish heart, true love, represents a mind-to-mind, face-to-face, eye-to-eye, body-to-body, soul-to-soul connection.

---

4   See
<https://www.chabad.org/theJewishWoman/article_cdo/aid/424441/jewish/T he-Jewish-Heart.htm>.

In the same way that Moses spoke with God "face to face" in Exodus 33:11, Jacob "saw God face to face" in Genesis 32:30. Therefore, Jacob's "face to face" encounter with God is not to be understood literally, but rather, as a figurative reference to encountering God, who manifested himself to Jacob, but not in his full power and glory. Jacob did not literally see God's "face"; after all, the form of the omnipresent God cannot be contained in the body of the "man" that Jacob wrestled. Rather, Jacob encountered a manifestation of God that could have been Jesus or an angel or some other manifestation, but it was not God in his full form and Jacob did not witness God's literal face.

Revelation 22:3-5 speaks of a day when we will be in God's full presence, and we will see God in all of His glory. Every tear will be wiped away and all the questions we have will be satisfied. When that day comes, we will see God's face. Until then, we can speak with God "face to face" as one speaks to a friend, just as Jacob and Moses did, but we cannot see God's face.

d. Like Jacob, Manoah Saw a Manifestation of God, but He Believed He Saw the "Lord" (Jdg 13:3-24)

Like Jacob, Samson's father Manoah saw a manifestation of God, but Manoah believed he saw the "Lord" (Jdg 13:22). In fact, Manoah only saw an angel of the Lord, as is made clear by the preceding verses:

> Jdg 13:3 The angel of the LORD appeared to her and said, "You are barren and childless, but you are going to become pregnant and give birth to a son.
> Jdg 13:6 Then the woman went to her husband and told him, "A man of God came to me. He looked like an angel of God, very awesome. I didn't ask him where he came from, and he didn't tell me his name.
> Jdg 13:9 God heard Manoah, and the angel of God came again to the woman while she was out in the field.
> Jdg 13:13 The angel of the LORD answered, "Your wife must do all that I have told her."
> Jdg 13:15 Manoah said to the angel of the LORD, "We would like you to stay until we prepare a young goat for you."

Jdg 13:16 The angel of the LORD replied, "Even though you detain me, I will not eat any of your food. But if you prepare a burnt offering, offer it to the LORD." (Manoah did not realize that it was the angel of the LORD.)
Jdg 13:17 Then Manoah inquired of the angel of the LORD, "What is your name, so that we may honor you when your word comes true?"
Jdg 13:18 He replied, "Why do you ask my name? It is beyond understanding."
Jdg 13:20 As the flame blazed up from the altar toward heaven, the angel of the LORD ascended in the flame.
Jdg 13:21 When the angel of the LORD did not show himself again to Manoah and his wife, Manoah realized that it was the angel of the LORD.

When Manoah proclaimed to his wife, "[w]e have seen God!" (Jdg 13:22), he was mistaken. If they had seen God, they would have died, for "no one may see me and live" (Exo 33:20). Manoah's wife, answering him, made clear that they would not die from seeing the appearance. She answered Manoah, saying, "If the LORD had meant to kill us, he would not have accepted a burnt offering and grain offering from our hands, nor shown us all these things or now told us this" (Jdg 13:23). The reason Manoah and his wife did not die is they did not see God. They saw only an "angel of the Lord." Manoah and his wife went on to live and gave birth to Samson (Jdg 13:24). Like Jacob, Manoah proclaimed that he saw God, but like Jacob, he did not see God in his full glory. Rather, he saw a partial manifestation of God. For Manoah, this partial manifestation took on the form of an "angel of the Lord." For Jacob, it took on the form of a "Man."

III. PROBLEM 3: JOHN STATES THAT NO MAN HAS SEEN GOD AT ANY TIME; THIS CANNOT BE TRUE IF JESUS IS GOD BECAUSE JESUS WAS SEEN

1. Overview

John writes in John 1:18:

NIV: John 1:18 No one has ever seen God, but the one and only Son, who is himself God and is in closest relationship with the Father, has made him known.

NKJV: John 1:18 No one has seen God at any time. The only begotten Son, who is in the bosom of the Father, He has declared Him.

However, Jesus was seen by many (the magi, his disciples, the witnesses to his resurrection, etc.). Therefore, if Jesus is God (John 1:1), then John was wrong because God was seen by all who saw Jesus.

2. Response: John's Deliberate Juxtaposition of the "Only Begotten Son" with "God" in John 1:18

John's deliberate juxtaposition of the "only begotten Son" with "God" in John 1:18 makes John's meaning very clear. He is not stating that no one has ever seen a manifestation of God. Clearly, Jesus was seen, and He is God. John knew that Jesus was God and the Son of God. John states just a few verses earlier that "[i]n the beginning was the Word, and the Word was with God, and the Word was God" (John 1:1). John's Gospel is filled with proclamations of Jesus's deity:

- John 1:49: Then Nathanael declared, "Rabbi, you are the Son of God; you are the king of Israel";
- John 11:27: "Yes, Lord," she replied, "I believe that you are the Messiah, the Son of God, who is to come into the world";
- John 19:7 "he claimed to be the Son of God";
- John 20:31 But these are written that you may believe that Jesus is the Messiah, the Son of God, and that by believing you may have life in his name.

John therefore knew that Jesus was the Son of God and one with God, and very obviously, Jesus had been seen, including by John. Therefore, when John stated that "[n]o one has seen God at any time," he could not have possibly meant that no one had seen Jesus, who was God's Son. Therefore, he was referring to God, the Godhead and Trinity, who is spirit (John 4:24) and, therefore, invisible. He was not referring to Jesus, "the image of the invisible God, the firstborn over all creation" (Col 1:15).

Jesus is the incarnation of the fullness of the Godhead, which chose Jesus, the name above all names, to represent it. All the fullness of the Godhead dwelt within Him, bodily. Jesus is God, but Jesus and God are not coterminous. Jesus is God in essence, but God is a trinity that consists of God the Father, God the Son and God the Holy Spirit. Therefore, John's juxtaposition of Jesus, who "declares" God and is seen, and God, who was never seen, makes clear that when John states that God was never seen, he is referring to God, as the Godhead, in His fullness and glory, not as the Son, who was seen; not as an angel speaking for God, who was seen; not as the manifestations of God made to Abraham, Hagar, Jacob, Manoah, Moses and other prophets and patriarchs; and not as a vision given to Micaiah, Isaiah, Daniel, Amos and other prophets. Rather, John is referring to God, in all of His fullness, who has never been seen.

IV. PROBLEM 4: JESUS SAYS TO THE PHARISEES "YOU HAVE NEITHER HEARD [THE FATHER'S] VOICE AT ANY TIME, NOR SEEN HIS FORM," BUT THE PHARISEES HEARD JESUS' VOICE AND SAW JESUS'S FORM

1. Overview

Jesus says to the Pharisees, "[y]ou have neither heard [the Father's] voice at any time, nor seen His form" (John 5:37). However, Jesus later states to Philip, "[h]e who has seen Me has seen the Father" (John 14:9). Therefore, anyone who has seen Jesus has seen the Father. Therefore, the Pharisees, who saw Jesus, saw the Father. Therefore, Jesus must have been mistaken when He said to the Pharisees that they had not heard the Father's voice or seen His form.

2. Response: There Is a Difference between Listening and Hearing and between Seeing and Perceiving

In John 5:37, Jesus is speaking to Pharisees who do not hear God's voice nor see God because they do not believe Jesus, whom God sent. To properly understand John 5:37, one should read:

- Isaiah 6:9, which distinguishes between seeing and perceiving: "Keep on hearing, but do not understand; Keep on seeing, but do not perceive" ("do not see" in the NIV); or
- Luke 8:10, where Jesus references the Scripture in Isaiah, stating, "To you [the disciples] it has been given to know the mysteries of the kingdom of God, but to the rest it is given in parables, that 'seeing they may not see, and hearing they may not understand."

Both the Pharisees and the disciples heard and saw Jesus, but only the disciples believed and were thus able to "hear" the Father's voice and "see" His form in the way Jesus meant.

CHAPTER 15. HAVE ALL SINNED (ROM 3:23) OR ARE THERE SOME WHO HAVE NOT SINNED ACCORDING TO THE LIKENESS OF ADAM (ROM 5:14)?

I. OVERVIEW

1. First, Romans States that All Have Sinned (Rom 3:23)

Paul writes in chapter 3 of the book of Romans:

Rom 3:23 for all have sinned and fall short of the glory of God,

2. Romans Then References Those Who did not Sin According to the Likeness of Adam's Transgression (Rom 5:14)

However, Paul later references "those who did not sin by breaking a command" in Romans chapter 5:

NKJV: Rom 5:14 Nevertheless death reigned from Adam to Moses, even over *those who had not sinned according to the likeness of the transgression of Adam*, who is a type of Him who was to come.
NIV: Rom 5:14 Nevertheless, death reigned from the time of Adam to the time of Moses, even over *those who did not sin by breaking a command*, as did Adam, who is a pattern of the one to come.

How can there be "those who did not sin by breaking a command" (Rom 5:14) if "all have sinned and fall short of the glory of God" (Rom 3:23)?

II. RESOLUTION

Romans 3:23 is referring to sin in a general sense. All
people have sinned in some way, and therefore fall short of the
glory of God (Rom 3:23). However, not all have sinned
specifically in the transgression of Adam, to which Roman 5:14
refers. Adam's sin was to break a command that was
specifically given to him by God:

> Gen 2:17 But of the tree of the knowledge of good and evil
> you shall not eat, for in the day that you eat of it you shall
> surely die."

God entered into a covenant with Adam and Eve based on
the condition of obedience. However, they disobeyed:

> Gen 3:6 So when the woman saw that the tree was good for
> food, that it was pleasant to the eyes, and a tree desirable to
> make one wise, she took of its fruit and ate. She also gave to
> her husband with her, and he ate.

Not all people have entered into a covenant with God and
not all people have received direct commandments from God.
Among those who have not entered into a covenant or received
direct commandments are Gentiles who have never received His
commandments or heard of Christ. In addition, it cannot be said
that a person who has not yet reached the age of accountability,
such as an infant, has sinned in the transgression of Adam. Such
a person may have sinned, but it is not the same as the
transgression of Adam, who received and knowingly disobeyed
a commandment of God.

In Romans 3, we learn that *all* people have sinned. In
Romans 5, we learn that the consequences of Adam's sin was
death over *all* of his progeny, not only those who sinned in the
likeness of his transgression (*i.e.*, by intentionally disobeying
his commandments). Paul writes:

> Rom 5:14 Nevertheless death reigned from Adam to Moses,
> even over those who had not sinned according to the likeness
> of the transgression of Adam, who is a type of Him who was
> to come.

Here, Paul anticipates the argument that those who came before Moses could not be under the condemnation of the law because there was no law before Moses, and unlike Adam, who willingly transgressed God's commandment, they did not receive commandments from God. Paul states that this does not matter. *All* of us are under the curse of sin, even those who did not transgress in the likeness of Adam:

> Rom 5:12 Therefore, just as through one man sin entered the world, and death through sin, and thus death spread to all men, because all sinned--
> Rom 5:13 (For until the law sin was in the world, but sin is not imputed when there is no law.
> Rom 5:14 Nevertheless death reigned from Adam to Moses, even over those who had not sinned according to the likeness of the transgression of Adam, who is a type of Him who was to come.

Therefore, there are two types of sin: (i) sin against the law (*i.e.*, of God's commandments), which is the type of sin that Adam committed; and (ii) the sin of those who do not have a law, but who commit sin nonetheless (*i.e.*, those who do not sin in the likeness of the transgression of Adam). Regardless of whether a person specifically sins in the likeness of Adam, he or she is under the reign of death and the judgment ushered in by sin.

CHAPTER 16. HOW MANY BLIND MEN DID JESUS ENCOUNTER WHEN LEAVING JERICHO?

I. OVERVIEW

- Two blind men
    - Mat 20:29 Now as they went out of Jericho, a great multitude followed Him. Mat 20:30 And behold, <u>two blind men</u> sitting by the road, when they heard that Jesus was passing by, cried out, saying, "Have mercy on us, O Lord, Son of David!"

- One blind man
    - Mark 10:46 Now they came to Jericho. As He went out of Jericho with His disciples and a great multitude, <u>blind Bartimaeus,</u> the son of Timaeus, sat by the road begging. Mark 10:47 And when he heard that it was Jesus of Nazareth, he began to cry out and say, "Jesus, Son of David, have mercy on me!"
    - Luke 18:35 Then it happened, as He was coming near Jericho, that a certain blind man sat by the road begging … Luke 18:38 And he cried out, saying, "Jesus, Son of David, have mercy on me!"

II. EXPLANATION

Matthew 20:29-30 makes it clear that as Jesus was leaving Jericho that there were two blind men sitting by the road. If there are two blind men, then there is certainly at least one there as well. The one focused on in Mark was Bartimeaus (Mark 10:46). Both called out for healing (Matthew 20:29-30). Perhaps Mark and Luke focus on Bartimeaus' account because he was the loudest and most determined, a point worth focusing on for spiritual reasons. God wants us to be persistent in laying our needs before Him.[5]

III. ANALYSIS

The discrepancy between the accounts in Matthew, on the one hand, and Mark and Luke, on the other, cannot, at first glance, be attributed to different focus or emphasis by the respective authors. In Matthew, two blind men cry out to Jesus, saying, "Have mercy on us, O Lord, Son of David!" However, in Mark and Luke, the one blind man (presumably Bartimeaus) cries out, saying, "Jesus, Son of David, have mercy on me!" If two blind men cried out, saying "Have mercy on us," then one of them could not have said, "have mercy on me." This appears to be a contradiction.

This contradiction would be resolved if two blind men were present and they cried out to Jesus, "have mercy on us" and one of them, Bartimeaus, separately cried out to Jesus, "have mercy on me." In this case, we could conclude that Matthew recounts both men's petition to Jesus and Mark and Luke recount only Bartimeaus's separate and distinct petition to Jesus. Bartimeaus could have said both "have mercy on us" and "have mercy on me," but each Gospel account only recounts one of these statements. This would make the discrepancy in the accounts not a contradiction, but a difference in focus and emphasis.

---

[5] This explanation is taken from the Christian Apologetics Research Ministry, available at https://carm.org/bible-difficulties/matthew-mark/how-many-blind-men-did-jesus-encounter-when-leaving-jericho.

CHAPTER 17. HOW MANY DEMON-POSSESSED MEN IN THE GERASENE TOMBS DID JESUS HEAL?

I. OVERVIEW

According to Matthew, there were two demon-possessed men. However, according to Mark and Luke, there was only one.

Matthew 8:28-34	Mark 5:1-20	Luke 8:26-39
Mat 8:28 When He had come to the other side, to the country of the Gergesenes, there met Him two demon-possessed men, coming out of the tombs, exceedingly fierce, so that no one could pass that way. Mat 8:29 And suddenly they cried out, saying, "What have we to do with You, Jesus, You Son of God? Have You come here to torment us before the time?" Mat 8:30 Now a	Mark 5:1 Then they came to the other side of the sea, to the country of the Gadarenes. Mark 5:2 And when He had come out of the boat, immediately there met Him out of the tombs a man with an unclean spirit, Mark 5:3 who had his dwelling among the tombs; and no one could bind him, not even with chains, Mark 5:4 because he had often been bound with shackles and	Luke 8:26 Then they sailed to the country of the Gadarenes, which is opposite Galilee. Luke 8:27 And when He stepped out on the land, there met Him a certain man from the city who had demons for a long time. And he wore no clothes, nor did he live in a house but in the tombs. Luke 8:28 When he saw Jesus, he cried out, fell down before Him, and with a loud voice said, "What have I to do with You,

good way off from them there was a herd of many swine feeding.

Mat 8:31 So the demons begged Him, saying, "If You cast us out, permit us to go away into the herd of swine."

Mat 8:32 And He said to them, "Go." So when they had come out, they went into the herd of swine. And suddenly the whole herd of swine ran violently down the steep place into the sea, and perished in the water.

Mat 8:33 Then those who kept them fled; and they went away into the city and told everything, including what had happened to the demon-possessed men.

Mat 8:34 And behold, the whole city came out to meet Jesus. And when they saw Him, they begged

chains. And the chains had been pulled apart by him, and the shackles broken in pieces; neither could anyone tame him.

Mark 5:5 And always, night and day, he was in the mountains and in the tombs, crying out and cutting himself with stones.

Mark 5:6 When he saw Jesus from afar, he ran and worshiped Him.

Mark 5:7 And he cried out with a loud voice and said, "What have I to do with You, Jesus, Son of the Most High God? I implore You by God that You do not torment me."

Mark 5:8 For He said to him, "Come out of the man, unclean spirit!"

Mark 5:9 Then He asked him, "What is your name?" And he answered, saying, "My name is Legion; for we

Jesus, Son of the Most High God? I beg You, do not torment me!"

Luke 8:29 For He had commanded the unclean spirit to come out of the man. For it had often seized him, and he was kept under guard, bound with chains and shackles; and he broke the bonds and was driven by the demon into the wilderness.

Luke 8:30 Jesus asked him, saying, "What is your name?" And he said, "Legion," because many demons had entered him.

Luke 8:31 And they begged Him that He would not command them to go out into the abyss.

Luke 8:32 Now a herd of many swine was feeding there on the mountain. So they begged Him that He would permit them to

Him to depart from their region.	are many."	enter them. And He permitted them.
	Mark 5:10 Also he begged Him earnestly that He would not send them out of the country.	Luke 8:33 Then the demons went out of the man and entered the swine, and the herd ran violently down the steep place into the lake and drowned.
	Mark 5:11 Now a large herd of swine was feeding there near the mountains.	
	Mark 5:12 So all the demons begged Him, saying, "Send us to the swine, that we may enter them."	Luke 8:34 When those who fed them saw what had happened, they fled and told it in the city and in the country.
	Mark 5:13 And at once Jesus gave them permission. Then the unclean spirits went out and entered the swine (there were about two thousand); and the herd ran violently down the steep place into the sea, and drowned in the sea.	Luke 8:35 Then they went out to see what had happened, and came to Jesus, and found the man from whom the demons had departed, sitting at the feet of Jesus, clothed and in his right mind. And they were afraid.
	Mark 5:14 So those who fed the swine fled, and they told it in the city and in the country. And they went out to see what it was that had	Luke 8:36 They also who had seen it told them by what means he who had been demon-possessed was healed.

	happened. Mark 5:15 Then they came to Jesus, and saw the one who had been demon-possessed and had the legion, sitting and clothed and in his right mind. And they were afraid. Mark 5:16 And those who saw it told them how it happened to him who had been demon-possessed, and about the swine. Mark 5:17 Then they began to plead with Him to depart from their region. Mark 5:18 And when He got into the boat, he who had been demon-possessed begged Him that he might be with Him. Mark 5:19 However, Jesus did not permit him, but said to him, "Go home to your friends, and tell them what great things the Lord has done for you, and	Luke 8:37 Then the whole multitude of the surrounding region of the Gadarenes asked Him to depart from them, for they were seized with great fear. And He got into the boat and returned. Luke 8:38 Now the man from whom the demons had departed begged Him that he might be with Him. But Jesus sent him away, saying, Luke 8:39 "Return to your own house, and tell what great things God has done for you." And he went his way and proclaimed throughout the whole city what great things Jesus had done for him.

	how He has had compassion on you." Mark 5:20 And he departed and began to proclaim in Decapolis all that Jesus had done for him; and all marveled.	

II. EXPLANATION

The first thing to determine is whether the three writers are describing the same event. The <u>timing</u> of the event in all three accounts—immediately <u>following the calming of the storm</u> on the sea of Galilee—as well as other similarities (living in the tombs, the ferocity of the demoniac, the conversation with the demons, the driving of them into the pigs, the drowning of the herd, and the response of those who witnessed the scene) all give credence to Matthew, Mark, and Luke all describing the same event. The question remains, then, whether there was one demoniac or two.[6]

Matthew tells us there were two demoniacs, while Mark and Luke only mention one of the two. It is unclear why they chose to mention only one, but that does not negate the possibility of a second demoniac being present. Mark and Luke do not say there was "only one" demon-possessed man. They simply state that one of the two met Jesus and spoke to Him. For whatever reason, Matthew simply gives us more information than Mark and Luke.[7]

---

[6] Taken from Got Questions, available at <https://www.gotquestions.org/one-two-demoniacs.html>.
[7] Taken from Got Questions, available at <https://www.gotquestions.org/one-two-demoniacs.html>.

Therefore, no contradiction exists. The fact that the three accounts differ in some minor details only proves that they were written by three different authors, each of whom chose to focus on a different aspect of the account.[8]

III. ANALYSIS

1. Overview

The discrepancy between the accounts in Matthew, on the one hand, and Mark and Luke, on the other, cannot, at first glance, be attributed to different focus or emphasis by the respective authors. In Matthew, two demon-possessed men cry out to Jesus, saying,

> Mat 8:29 And suddenly they cried out, saying, "What <u>have we</u> to do with You, Jesus, You Son of God? Have You come here to torment <u>us</u> before the time?"

In Mark and Luke, in contrast, a single demon-possessed man is reported to have said:

> Mark 5:7 And he cried out with a loud voice and said, "What have I to do with You, Jesus, Son of the Most High God? I implore You by God that You do not torment me."
> Luke 8:28 When he saw Jesus, he cried out, fell down before Him, and with a loud voice said, "What have I to do with You, Jesus, Son of the Most High God? I beg You, <u>do not torment me</u>!"

2. First Possibility: Both Men Were Together, but One of Them Cried Out to Jesus Separately

This appears to be a contradiction. However, the contradiction would be resolved if two demon-possessed men were present and they cried out to Jesus, "What <u>have we</u> to do with You ... Have You come here to torment <u>us</u>" before one of them separately cried out, "What have I to do with You ... <u>do not torment me</u>." In this case, we could conclude that Matthew

---

[8]   Taken   from   Got   Questions,   available   at <https://www.gotquestions.org/one-two-demoniacs.html>.

recounts both men's petition to Jesus, whereas Mark and Luke recount only one man's separate and distinct petition to Jesus. One of the demon-possessed men could have said both "What have we to do with You," with "we" meaning the demon-possessed man and the second demon-possessed man, or meaning the legion of demons (in the plural), and then subsequently said "What have I to do with You," referring to him singularly, but with Mark and Luke recounting only the singular renditions and Matthew rendering the plural. This would make the discrepancy in the accounts not a contradiction, but a difference in focus and emphasis.

3. Second Possibility: The Quotation Marks Are Not Meant to Record Literal Meanings in the Original Greek

A second way to reconcile the apparent contradiction is to read the quotation marks we find in modern English translations as absent in the original Greek texts (both the Hebrew Old Testament and Greek New Testament do not include quotation marks).[9] This is because the biblical writers did not intend to give exact quotes of each word spoken. The insertion of quotation marks in modern translations gives the false impression that authors quoted word-for-word, which is not the case. When reading the Scriptures, we should recognize the *ideas* that are put forward, not the word-for-word texts, which in many cases are compromised in translation. Although their exact word-for-word presentation may vary, the ideas put forward by different accounts of the same event are always consistent with one another.

---

[9] The King James Version of the Bible, recognizing this truth, does not insert quotes in its translation..

CHAPTER 18. INCONSISTENCIES BETWEEN 2 SAMUEL AND 1 CHRONICLES

I. HORSEMEN TAKEN BY DAVID (2SA 8 AND 1CH 18)

2Sa 8:4 David took from him one thousand chariots, **seven hundred horsemen**, and twenty thousand foot soldiers. Also David hamstrung all the chariot horses, except that he spared enough of them for one hundred chariots.	Explanation 1[10]: It is likely that 1Ch uses a different numbering system than 2Sa. Whereas 1Ch is counting the horsemen, 2Sa is probably counting the *companies* of horseman (*i.e.,* 700 companies of 10 horsemen each, for a total of 7,000 horsemen). The flaw in this explanation is that 2 Samuel clearly states 700 "horsemen," not 700 "companies of horsemen."
1Ch 18:4 David took from him one thousand chariots, **seven thousand horsemen**, and twenty thousand foot soldiers. Also David hamstrung all the chariot horses, except that he spared enough of them for one hundred chariots.	Explanation 2[11]: An explanation offered by Gerardus D. Bouw in The Book of Bible Problems. He says on page 84: "Apparently the 6,300 were captured as a group while the remaining 700 were captured at a different time. In support of this theory he notes the differences in the language used in the two

[10] http://thebereans.net/contra-r08.shtml.
[11] From http://www.blessedquietness.com/journal/resource/contrdct.htm.

sections.

In II Samuel 8:3 it says David smote Hadadezer as he went *to recover* his border at the river Euphrates, while in I Chronicles 18:3 it says David smote Hadarezer as he went *to establish* his dominion by the river Euphrates.

So, in effect he is suggesting that Hadarezar initially went to stabilize his control over the Euphrates and David took his troops of 700 horsemen. Then Hadarezar sent another 6300 to recover his previous dominion and then these too were taken by David, thus making a total of 7,000.

Explanation 3[12]:

An important part of the equation is that some footmen were also horsemen; they could either fight on horse or on foot since they were specifically trained for both methods of combat. Those footmen who were also horsemen could then replace the number of fallen horsemen in the midst of battle. We see this double role in another passage. In 2 Samuel 10:18 we are told of 40,000 HORSEMEN of the Syrian army who were slain by king

---

[12] From http://www.blessedquietness.com/journal/resource/contrdct.htm.

David and his men; but in 1 Chronicles 19:18 this same number is listed as 40,000 FOOTMEN. These particular soldiers could fight either on foot or on horseback.

When we compare 2 Samuel 8:4 - the 700 horsemen taken with the number of 7000 horsemen taken in battle in I Chronicles 18:4, the difference can be attributed to how each writer is considering the men in question. The additional 6, 300 men were trained as both horsemen and footsoldiers. As "horsemen" reserves they could be included with the 700 and so would be combined as a total of 7000, but as footsoldiers they would be counted among the 20,000.

So how many "horsemen" were slain? Seven hundred - but also an additional 6,300 who were trained both as horsemen and footmen. The two different writers are giving two different views of the same events.

However, if the Chronicles account were counting 6,300 foot solders who were also trained as horsemen in the horsemen category, then it should state that 13,700 foot soldiers were slain, no?

II. CHARIOTEERS AND HORSEMEN KILLED BY DAVID (2SA 10 AND 1CH 19)

2Sa 10:18 Then the Syrians fled before Israel; and David killed **seven hundred charioteers** and **forty thousand horsemen** of the Syrians, and struck **Shobach** the commander of their army, who died there.	Regarding the 700 charioteers: It is possible that 2 Samuel refers to the men in 700 chariots and 1 Chronicles refers to 7,000 men in chariots (*i.e.*, there were about 10 men in each chariot). However, this interpretation is not supported by the text.
1Ch 19:18 Then the Syrians fled before Israel; and David killed **seven thousand charioteers** and **forty thousand foot soldiers** of the Syrians, and killed **Shophach** the commander of the army.	Regarding the 40,000 horsemen / foot solders: It is entirely conceivable that the 40,000 horsemen were also foot soldiers.

III. WHETHER MICHAL HAD CHILDREN (2SA 6 AND 2SA 23)

2Sa 6:23 Therefore Michal the daughter of Saul had no children to the day of her death.	This can be explained by a translation error. Although the KJV, MKJV and NKJV refer to "Michal the daughter of Saul" in 2Sa 21:8, the ISV, NIV and many other editions refer to the five sons of "Merab," the daughter of Saul, whom she had borne to Adriel, who was her husband according to 1Sa 18:19. It would not make sense that 2Sa 21:8 refer to Michal because she was *not* Adriel's wife.
2Sa 21:8 So the king took Armoni and Mephibosheth, the two sons of Rizpah the daughter of Aiah, whom she bore to Saul, and the five sons of Michal the daughter of Saul, whom she brought up for Adriel the son of Barzillai the Meholathite.	The reason why some

	translations, including the KJV, refer to Michael rather than Merab in 2Sa 21:8, is that the Septuagint (the Greek translation of the Hebrew) as well as all but two Hebrew manuscripts, refer to "Michal." However, it would appear that "Merab" was referenced in the original, since she was Adriel's wife. The reference to "Michael" is most likely an ancient scribal error.[13] In either case, even if it was "Michal" referred to in 2Sa 21:8, the verse states that the five sons were "brought up for Adriel." It is thus possible that they were only her "sons" in a "surrogate" rather than biological sense.

IV. THE PLAGUES OF ISRAEL: THREE YEARS OR SEVEN YEARS? (2SA 24, 1CH 21)

1. Overview

a. 2 Samuel Account

2 Samuel gives an account of 7 years of famine, as follows:

- An initial 3 years (due to "Saul and his bloodthirsty house");
- A buffer between the initial 3 years and the initiation of the census (presumably 2 months and 10 days);

---

[13] See http://carm.org/bible-difficulties/joshua-esther/did-michal-have-any-children-or-not.

- Followed by 9 months and 20 days (nearly 1 year) (for taking the census);
- Plus 3 additional years offered as presented in 1 Chronicles 21:12 (as punishment for taking the census).

b. 1 Chronicles Account

1 Chronicles, in contrast, gives an account of 3 years of famine:

Event no.	2 Samuel	1 Chronicles
1	2Sa 21:1 Now there was a famine in the days of David for three years, year after year; and David inquired of the LORD. And the LORD answered, "It is because of Saul and his bloodthirsty house, because he killed the Gibeonites.	NA
2	[There is a buffer here between event 1 and 3, to allow the events of 2Sa 22 and 23 (e.g., the killing of the Philistines (2Sa 23:12)) to transpire. It presumably takes 2 months and 10 days to equal the full 7 years.]	NA
3	2Sa 24:8 So when they had gone through all the land, they came to Jerusalem at the end of nine months and twenty days [for taking the census]. 2Sa 24:9 Then Joab gave the sum of the number of	NA 1Ch 21:5 Then Joab gave the sum of the number of the people to David. All Israel had one million one hundred thousand men who drew the sword, and Judah had four hundred and seventy thousand men

	the people [*i.e.*, the census results] to the king. And there were in Israel <u>eight hundred thousand</u> valiant men who drew the sword, and the men of Judah were <u>five hundred thousand</u> men.	who drew the sword. 1Ch 21:6 But he <u>did not count Levi and Benjamin</u> among them, for the king's word was abominable to Joab.
4	2Sa 24:13 [after discussing the 3 years of famine that already passed and the 9 months and 20 days for taking the census]: So Gad came to David and told him; and he said to him, "Shall seven years[14] of famine come to you in your land? Or shall you flee three months before your enemies, while they pursue you? Or shall there be three days' plague in your land? Now consider and see what answer I should take back to Him who sent me."	1Ch 21:12: "Thus says the LORD: 'Choose for yourself, either three years of famine, or three months to be defeated by your foes with the sword of your enemies overtaking you, or else for three days the sword of the LORD—the plague in the land, with the angel of the LORD destroying throughout all the territory of Israel.' Now consider what answer I should take back to Him who sent me."

c. Discrepancies between Translations of 2 Samuel 24:13

To further complicate this issue, there are discrepancies between how various translations of the Bible have translated 2 Samuel 24:13. Some of them have translated the reference to the years as 7 years, while others have translated it as 3 years.

---

[14] Note, this is translated as 3 years in the NIV and the Bible in Basic English, and 7 years in the KJV, NKJ, French Darby, Biblia de las Américas, French Lous Segond, International Standard Version, Spanish Sagradas Escrituras, Arabic Smith and Van Dyke, and the Turkish Kutsal Kitap.

- "3 years" is provided in the following translations:
  o NIV
  o Bible in Basic English

- "7 years" is provided in the following translations:
  o KJV
  o NKJV
  o French Darby
  o Biblia de las Américas
  o French Louis Segond
  o International Standard Version
  o Spanish Sagradas Escrituras
  o Arabic Smith & Van Dyke
  o Turkish Kutsal Kitap

2. Explanation 1: 2 Samuel Adds Four Years of Initial Famine to the Three Additional Years Offered

a. Overview

Several web sites, including "7 years or 3 years of famine?"[15] give the following explanation:

In reality, Gad offered David 3 years of famine in addition to the 4 that had already transpired by that point. 2 Samuel gives an account of the 4 years that had already transpired and the 3 additional years for a total of 7 years, which are offered to David; 1 Chronicles gives the account of *only* the 3 additional years of famine.

In 2Sa 21:1, we read: "Now there was a famine in the days of David for three years, year after year."

Thereafter, in 2Sa 24:8, we read, "So when they had gone through all the land, they came to Jerusalem at the end of nine months and twenty days."

The only way to reconcile this apparent contradiction, as well as that recorded in the Exodus 20 and Deuteronomy 5 accounts, is to recognize that the quotation marks we find in

---

15

http://blessedquietness.com/journal/housechu/three_years_or_seven_years_o f_famine.htm.

many modern translations do not exist in the original texts (both the Hebrew Old Testament and Greek New Testament do not include quotation marks).[16] This is because the biblical writers did not intend to give exact quotes of each word spoken. The insertion of quotation marks in modern translations give the false idea that authors quoted word-for-word, which is not the case. When reading the Scriptures, we should recognize the *ideas* that are poured forward. Although their exact word-for-word presentation may vary, the ideas put forward by different accounts of the same event are always consistent with one another.

b. Potential Issue with this Explanation

The only potential issue with this explanation is that it assumes, without any apparent evidence, that the famine continued in the period between:

-   The first three years of famine; and
-   God's offer to David of new famine of three years (for a total of seven).

In other words, a famine continued during the following periods:

-   The three years of famine;
-   During the killing of the Philistines (2Sa 23:12), which would have had to have taken two months and ten days;
-   The nine months and twenty days for taking the census (2Sa 24:8).

This would have equaled a total of four years, which, when added to the additional three years referenced in 1 Chronicles, would come out to a total of seven years.

However, we do not know whether the famine continued during the killing of the Philistines in 2 Samuel 23:12 or in the nine months and twenty days for taking the census in 2 Samuel 24:8.

---

[16] The King James Version of the Bible, recognizing this truth, does not insert quotes in its translation..

3. Explanation 2: Translators' Error

The Treasury of Scriptural Knowledge provides the following commentary on 1 Chronicles 21:12:

> three years' famine: In 2Sa_24:13, it is <u>seven years</u>; but the [Greek] Septuagint has there τρια ετη [Strong's G5140], three years, as here; which is, no doubt, the true reading; the letter ז, zayin, seven, being mistaken for ג, gimmel, three. Lev_26:26-29; 2Sa_21:1, 2Sa_24:13; 1Ki_17:1; 2Ki_8:1; Lam_4:9; Luk_4:25

If we accept this explanation, we can conclude that the KJV and several other English translations of the Bible mistook the Hebrew ג, gimmel, three for the letter ז, zayin, seven when preparing their translations. In other words, the translators of the Bible into English were not infallible.

4. Conclusion

According to the explanations proposed above, we can conclude that one of the following is true:

- The authors of the KJV and other translations of the Bible that use seven years in 2 Samuel 24:13 mistook the Hebrew ג, gimmel, three for the letter ז, zayin, seven; or
- The author of the original Hebrew manuscript of 2 Samuel 24:13 did in fact use the Hebrew letter ז, zayin, seven, but in so doing, he was counting the three years of initial famine recounted in 2 Samuel 21:1 plus the 9 months and 20 days for taking the census in 2 Samuel 24:8.

Neither of these explanations poses a grave problem or threat to the integrity of the Bible. Mistaking a number is an innocent error with no grave consequences that does not cast into question the overall message of the Bible; if anything, it simply reinforces the biblical teaching that man is imperfect and that only God is infallible; the translators of the Bible, like all men, are fallible. That they might make a mistake in translating the text does not cast into doubt the validity of the original text.

The alternate explanation simply shows that different books of the Bible propose using different counting methodologies, with one book (2 Samuel) choosing to aggregate the total number of years of famine and the second book (1 Chronicles) choosing instead to highlight only the additional time (3 years) being aggregated to the past famine.

CHAPTER 19. IS GOD OR SATAN THE RULER OF THIS WORLD, WITH AUTHORITY OVER GOVERNMENTS?

I. EVIDENCE THAT SATAN RULES THE WORLD (JESUS, PAUL, JOHN)

1. **Satan is the "ruler of this world" (John 12:30-31, 14:30, 16:7) (Jesus).**
   - John 12:30 Jesus said ... John 12:31 Now is the judgment of this world; now the *ruler of this world* will be cast out.
   - John 14:30 I will no longer talk much with you, for the *ruler of this world* is coming, and he has nothing in Me.
   - John 16:7 Nevertheless I tell you the truth. It is to your advantage that I go away; for if I do not go away, the Helper will not come to you; but if I depart, I will send Him to you. John 16:8 And when He has come, He will convict the world of sin, and of righteousness, and of judgment ... John 16:11 of judgment, because the *ruler of this world* is judged.

2. **Satan is the "god of this age" (2Co 4:4) (Paul).**
   - 2Co 4:4 whose minds the god of this age has blinded, who do not believe, lest the light of the gospel of the glory of Christ, who is the image of God, should shine on them.

3. **Satan is the "prince of the power of the air" (Eph 2:2) (Paul).**
   - Eph 2:2 in which you once walked according to the course of this world, according to the *prince of the power of the air*, the spirit who now works in the sons of disobedience.

4. **The whole world lies "under the sway" of Satan (1Jn 5:19) (John)**

   - 1Jn 5:19 We know that we are of God, and the whole world lies under the sway of the wicked one.

II. EVIDENCE THAT SEEMS TO SUGGEST THAT SATAN RULES THE WORLD (SATAN)

1. Satan offered all of the kingdoms of the world because they belonged to him; Jesus did not deny this.

   - Mat 4:8 Again, the devil took Him up on an exceedingly high mountain, and showed Him all the kingdoms of the world and their glory. Mat 4:9 And he said to Him, "All these things I will give You if You will fall down and worship me."
   - Luke 4:6 And the devil said to Him, "All this authority I will give You, and their glory; for this has been delivered to me, and I give it to whomever I wish.

2. Inadequacy of Argument

This argument is, however, inadequate because it assumes that Satan was not lying when he said "[a]ll this authority … has been delivered to me" (Luke 4:6). While Jesus did not specifically dispute this claim, we must remember when weighing any of Satan's words that he "does not stand in the truth, because there is no truth in him. When he speaks a lie, he speaks from his own resources, for he is a liar and the father of it" (John 8:44).

III. EVIDENCE THAT GOD HOLDS ALL AUTHORITY OVER THE WORLD (PAUL, PETER)

1. Melchizedek was ruler of Salem and was a priest of God, thus under God's authority (Moses)

Melchizedek was "king of Salem" and, at the same, time, "the priest of God Most High" (Gen 14:18). It would be inconceivable and incongruous that Melchizedek, who had authority over Salem and was a priest of God, would be under Satan's authority rather than God's.

2. The Epistles state that all authority is in Jesus (Paul, Peter).

- God sat Jesus "at His right hand in the heavenly places, far above all principality and power and might and dominion, and every name that is named, not only in this age but also in that which is to come. And He put *all things under His feet* (Eph 1:20-22).
- Jesus is "the head of all principality and power" (Col 2:10).
- Jesus is at the "right hand of God, angels and *authorities and powers* having been made subject to Him" (1Pe 3:22).

3. There is "no authority except from God"; the civil authority is "appointed by God" as God's "minister," bearing "the sword" to exact vengeance on him "who practices evil" (Rom 13:1-4) (Paul).

Paul's letter to the Romans, which states that the civil authority is "appointed by God" (Rom 13:1), equates the civil authority with God's "ordinance" (Rom 13:2) and states that the civil authority is "God's minister" (Rom 13:4):

- Rom 13:1 Let every soul be subject to the governing authorities. *For there is no authority except from God, and the authorities that exist are appointed by God.*
- Rom 13:2 Therefore whoever resists the authority resists the ordinance of God, and those who resist will bring judgment on themselves.
- Rom 13:3 For rulers are not a terror to good works, but to evil. Do you want to be unafraid of the authority? Do what is good, and you will have praise from the same.
- Rom 13:4 For he is God's *minister* to you for good. But if you do evil, be afraid; for he does not bear the *sword* in vain; for he is God's minister, an avenger to execute wrath on *him who practices evil.*

The fact that civil authorities are "appointed by God" (Rom 13:1) clearly indicates that they are under God. It is thus God, not Satan, that holds all authority over the world.

4. Christians are to pay taxes to and pray for the civil authority (Rom 13:6-7; 1Ti 2:1-2) (Paul).

We are therefore to support the authorities by paying taxes (Rom 13:6-7):

- Rom 13:6 For because of this you also pay taxes, for they are God's ministers attending continually to this very thing.
- Rom 13:7 Render therefore to all their due: taxes to whom taxes are due, customs to whom customs, fear to whom fear, honor to whom honor.

We are also to pray for our rulers (1Ti 2:1-2):

- 1Ti 2:1 Therefore I exhort first of all that supplications, prayers, intercessions, and giving of thanks be made for all men,
- 1Ti 2:2 for kings and all who are in authority, that we may lead a quiet and peaceable life in all godliness and reverence.

IV. EXPLANATIONS OF APPARENT CONTRADICTION

1. Alternative 1: Satan Once Had Dominion over the World, but on the Cross, Jesus Took This Authority from Him

a. Explanation

Prior to the death and resurrection of Jesus on the cross, Satan was the ruler of the world. He had dominion over man, who was through sin condemned. Satan thus offered to Jesus all of the kingdoms of the world because at that time, prior to Jesus' death and resurrection, they all belonged to him (Jesus thus never disputed this point). Similarly, prior to his death and resurrection, Jesus repeated many times over that Satan was the "ruler of this world." Yet He said that Satan, the "ruler of this world," will be "cast out" (John 12:30) and is "judged" (John 16:11). Here, Jesus is referring to the day that was coming in which He vanquishes sin and death through His resurrection on the cross. On that day, Satan would be "cast out" and would lose his dominion over the world; Jesus would be given all authority, and after His resurrection, His parting words are: "All authority has been given to Me in heaven and on earth" (Mat 28:18).

In the post-resurrection epoch, the civil authority is "appointed by God" (Rom 13:1) and is "God's minister" (Rom 13:4), to which we must pay taxes (Rom 13:6-7) and for which we are to pray (1Ti 2:1-2).

b. Inadequacy of Explanation

This explanation is inadequate for the following reasons:

-   It fails to address Paul's Epistles, which were written after Jesus' death and resurrection and yet refer to Satan as the "god of this age" (2Co 4:4) and state that the whole world lies under his "sway" (1Jn 5:19);
-   The argument assumes that within just a few years after the resurrection of Christ, all governments would have been redeemed and, whereas before the resurrection, they were all corrupt and under Satan's dominion, they were after the resurrection restored to Christ and thus could receive Christians' support through taxes (Rom 13:6-7) and prayer (1Ti 2:1-2). However, the reality is that for 300 years after the resurrection of Christ, the government that ruled over the Christians was a brutal empire that persecuted the Christians and fed them to the lions.

2. Alternative 2: Satan Controls Civil Authorities, But God Controls Satan

a. Explanation

God, who holds *ultimate* authority over all of creation, has allowed Satan, the "ruler of this world" (John 12:30-31; John

14:30; John 16:7-11), to rule over governments and kingdoms. Satan has the power to mete out this authority to whomever he pleases. Civil rulers are thus given their authority by Satan, who controls the world, but it is God, who has ultimate authority and indirectly "appoints" the authorities by allowing Satan to mete out his power (Rom 13:1).

b. Inadequacy of Explanation

This explanation fails to address the apparent contradiction between Jesus' reference to Satan as the "ruler of this world" (John 12:30-31; John 14:30; John 16:7-11) and the simultaneous repeated references to all authority being under Jesus (1Pe 3:22; Eph 1:20-22). Moreover, calling Satan's "ruler of this world" cannot be reconciled with Romans 13:1-4, which states that the civil authorities are "appointed" by God as His "minister."

3. **Alternative 3: Satan's Control Is Limited to the Sphere of Sin; God Holds Ultimate Control over Satan and the Civil Authorities**

a. Explanation

Paul writes in 2 Corinthians and Ephesians:

-   Satan is the "god of this age" (2Co 4:4) (Paul).
-   Satan is the "prince of the power of the air" (Eph 2:2) (Paul).

These verses are not stating that Satan is the ruler of civil authorities or appoints them. Rather, he is reiterating what John writes in 1 John: "the whole world lies under the sway of the wicked one" (1Jn 5:19). In other words, Satan has "sway" or influence over the whole world. This influence is comprised of tempting the world into sin and corrupting all of creation with the consequences of sin (*e.g.*, sickness, pain, suffering , death).

Paul then writes in Colossians and Romans:

-   Jesus is "the head of all principality and power" (Col 2:10) (Paul).

- The civil authority is "appointed by God" as God's "minister," bearing "the sword" to exact vengeance on he "who practices evil" (Rom 13:1-4) (Paul).
- Christians are to pay taxes to and pray for the civil authority (Rom 13:6-7; 1Ti 2:1-2) (Paul).

These verses, in contrast, refer to true civil authority, not just the power to tempt people into sin. They make clear that all authority ultimately resides in Christ and that God uses the civil authority as His minister to exact justice.

b. Empirical Evidentiary Problem: If Civil Authorities are God's "Ministers," then Aren't their Evil Deeds Committed on God's Behalf?

The fact that governments are so evil makes it very difficult to accept that God rather than Satan ultimately controls civil authorities and "appoints" them as His "minister" (Rom 13:1-4). After all, governments were responsible for the throwing of Israel's newborn babies into the river (Exo 1:22), putting to death the male children in Bethlehem (Mat 2:16), crucifying Jesus (Mat 27:17-25) and stoning Stephen (Acts 7:59) and other martyrs.

In modern days, we continue to see that some of the worst atrocities and evils are committed by the very governments that are supposed to be "avenger[s] to execute wrath on him who practices evil" (Rom 13:4). We live in a world marked by genocide, crimes against humanity and war crimes committed at the hands of governments, including Hitler's Germany and Milosevic's Serbia. This empirical evidence suggests that the world is under the authority of Satan, rather than God.

c. Response to Empirical Evidentiary Problem: The Scriptures Do Not Claim that Civil Authorities Are Without Corruption; In Any Case, God Uses the Evils of the Civil Authorities that He Appoints to Realize His Plans

a. *The Scriptures Do Not Claim that Civil Authorities Are Without Corruption*

The Scriptures never claim that civil authorities are without corruption. Rather, they state that the civil authorities are "appointed by God" (Rom 13:4). Yet like every other part of creation, civil authorities are subject to the corrupting influence of sin. They have, for example, abused their divinely-mandated authority, committing atrocities against their own people and aggressing against other nations. Rather than using their swords to punish evil, they commit evils. Thus, like the rest of creation, the civil authorities are under Satan's "sway" (1Jn 5:19).

b.   In Any Case, God Uses the Evils of the Civil Authorities that He Appoints to Realize His Plans

Just because governments commit evil does not mean that they are not "appointed by God" as God's "minister" (Rom 13:1-4). God can use the evils of governments to realize His plans. For example, God allowed Pharaoh's evils and hardened heart so that He would send plagues to make it known that "there is none like [God] in all the earth" (Exo 9:14) and to "show [God's] power" so that His name "may be declared in all the earth" (Exo 9:16). Moreover, God allowed the Roman government to torture and crucify Jesus, an innocent man, in order to set into motion His resurrection and the redemption of all of mankind. In this same vein, the attempted genocide of the Jewish people in Nazi Germany served as the impetus for the establishment of the modern State of Israel.

CHAPTER 20. NUMBER OF SYRIAN CHARIOTEERS WHO DIED IN BATTLE WITH DAVID

I. OVERVIEW

The author of 2 Samuel states that <u>700</u> Syrian charioteers died during a battle with David, while the author of 1 Chronicles states that <u>7,000</u> charioteers died:

> 2Sa 10:18 Then the Syrians fled before Israel; and David killed <u>seven hundred charioteers</u> and forty thousand horsemen of the Syrians, and struck Shobach the commander of their army, who died there.
> 1Ch 19:18 Then the Syrians fled before Israel; and David killed <u>seven thousand charioteers</u> and forty thousand foot soldiers of the Syrians, and killed Shophach the commander of the army.

II. PROPOSED EXPLANATION 1: 2 SAMUEL REFERS TO 700 CHARIOTS AND 1 CHRONICLES REFERS TO 7,000 CHARIOTEERS

1. Overview

It is possible that 2 Samuel refers to 700 chariots and 1 Chronicles refers to 7,000 men in chariots (*i.e.*, with about 10 men in each chariot). The word for charioteers used in 2 Samuel and 1 Chronicles is Strong's H7393, which Strong's Definitions defines as:

> רֶכֶב rekeb, reh'-keb; from H7392; a <u>vehicle</u>; by <u>implication, a team</u>; by extension, cavalry; by analogy a rider, i.e. the upper millstone:—chariot, (upper) millstone, multitude (from the margin), wagon.

The meaning of the Hebrew רֶכֶב can apply to both a vehicle as well as a team (i.e., it can mean both a chariot as well as the team of riders in the chariot). It is thus possible that 2 Samule, in employing the Hebrew רֶכֶב, was referring to the number of chariots that perished at the hands of David, whereas 1 Chronicles referred to the 7,000 men in the 700 chariots that perished. Under this reading, the number preceding the word "charioteer" should not be viewed as a contradiction.

2. Scriptural Renditions

a. KJV

The KJV translates the texts as follows:

2Sa 10:18 And the Syrians fled before Israel; and David slew *the men of* seven hundred chariots of the Syrians, and forty thousand horsemen, and smote Shobach the captain of their host, who died there.
1Ch 19:18 But the Syrians fled before Israel; and David slew of the Syrians *seven thousand men* which fought in chariots, and forty thousand footmen, and killed Shophach the captain of the host.

b. MKJV

The MKJV translates the texts as follows:

2Sa 10:18 And the Syrians fled before Israel. And David killed *the men of* seven hundred chariots of the Syrians, and forty thousand horsemen, and struck Shobach the captain of their army, who died there.
1Ch 19:18 But the Syrians fled before Israel. And David killed *seven thousand of the Syrians in chariots*, and forty thousand footmen; and he killed Shophach the commander of the army.

c. NKJV

The NKJV translates the texts as follows:

2Sa 10:18 Then the Syrians fled before Israel; and David killed *seven hundred charioteers* and forty thousand horsemen of the Syrians, and struck Shobach the commander of their army, who died there.

1Ch 19:18 Then the Syrians fled before Israel; and David killed *seven thousand charioteers* and forty thousand foot soldiers of the Syrians, and killed Shophach the commander of the army.

3. Problem with the Proposed Explanation: David Cannot "Kill" a Chariot

The problem with the proposed explanation is that it would make little sense if we read 2 Samuel 10:18 to mean that David "killed" seven hundred chariots. A chariot is a vehicle that cannot be killed.

The KJV and MKJV resolve this issue by adding in italics the words *"the men of"* before the words "seven hundred chariots" in 2 Samuel 2:18. This thus makes clear that what the author of 2 Samuel 10:18 meant was that David killed the charioteers, not the chariots. However, this does not resolve the contradiction with 1 Chronical 19:18 because the KJV and MKJV also add in their translations of 1 Chronicles 19:18 that David slew "seven thousand men which fought in chariots" in the KJV and "seven thousand of the Syrians in chariots" in the MKJV, thus reverting to the contradiction between 2 Samuel 10:18 and 1 Chronicles 19:18.

4. Answer to the Problem with the Proposed Explanation

The issue with the KJV and MKJV translations of 2 Samuel 10:18 and 1 Chronicles 19:18 is that it fails to take into account that the Hebrew הָרַג (hârag) and רֶכֶב (rekeb) can be translated in more than one way in English. As discussed above, רֶכֶב (rekeb) can mean both a chariot and the team of charioteers that ride in chariots. Moreover, the word translated as "slew" in the KJV and "killed" in the MKJV, הָרַג (hârag), can mean both kill and destroy. The original Hebrew uses Strong's H2026, defined by Strong's Definitions as:

הָרַג hârag, haw-rag'; a primitive root; to smite with deadly intent:—destroy, out of hand, kill, murder(-er), put to (death), make (slaughter), slay(-er), × surely.

Given this broad definition, 2 Samuel 10:18 can be read to mean that David "destroyed" 700 chariots, which is consistent with the statement in 1 Chronicles 19:18 that David killed 7,000 charioteers.

In other words, it is entirely possible that 2 Samuel 10:18, though it is using the same Hebrew הָרַג (hârag) and רֶכֶב (rekeb) as 1 Chronicles 19:18, is referring <u>not</u> to the killing of charioteers, but rather, to the destruction of chariots, while 1 Chronicles 19:18 is referring to the killing of charioteers, with teams of approximately 10 soldiers (the rough equivalent to a modern military squadron) riding in each chariot. Modern translations of the Bible, viewing the words Hebrew הָרַג (hârag) and רֶכֶב (rekeb) that are used in the original Hebrew of 2 Samuel 10:18 and 1 Chronicles 19:18, have used the same English renditions in their translations of 2 Samuel 10:18 and 1 Chronicles 19:18, which leads to a contradiction, whereas the original Hebrew of these terms is subject to more than one meaning.

CHAPTER 21. NUMBER OF TIMES THE ROOSTER CROWED BEFORE PETER DENIED JESUS THREE TIMES

I. TEXTS

1. Twice According to Mark

Jesus said to Peter, "Assuredly, I say to you that today, even this night, before the rooster crows twice, you will deny Me three times" (Mark 14:30).

a. First Accusation; First Denial; First Crowing of the Rooster

One of the servant girls of the high priest saw Peter warming himself and said, "You also were with Jesus of Nazareth" (Mark 14:67). He denied it, saying, "I neither know nor understand what you are saying." And he went out on the porch, and *a rooster crowed* (Mark 14:68).

b. Second Accusation; Second Denial

The servant girl saw him again, and began to say to those who stood by, "This is one of them" (Mark 14:69). He denied it again (Mark 14:70).

c. Third Accusation; Third Denial; Second crowing of the Rooster

A little later those who stood by said to Peter again, "Surely you are one of them; for you are a Galilean, and your speech shows it" (Mark 14:70).

Peter began to "curse and swear, 'I do not know this Man of whom you speak!' (Mark 14:71).

"A second time the rooster crowed" (Mark 14:72).

2. Once According to Matthew, Luke and John

a. Matthew

Jesus said to Peter, "Assuredly, I say to you that this night, before the rooster crows, you will deny Me three times" (Mat 26:34).

"Then he began to curse and swear, saying, 'I do not know the Man!' Immediately a rooster crowed. And Peter remembered the word of Jesus who had said to him, 'Before the rooster crows, you will deny Me three times.' So he went out and wept bitterly" (Mat 26:74-75).

b. Luke

Jesus said, "I tell you, Peter, the rooster shall not crow this day before you will deny three times that you know Me" (Luke 22:34).

c. John

Jesus said to Peter, "Most assuredly, I say to you, the rooster shall not crow till you have denied Me three times" (John 13:38).

"Peter then denied again; and immediately a rooster crowed" (John 18:27).

II. CHARTS

1. Map of Mark

a. Jesus' Prediction (Mark 14:30)

Mark 14:30 Jesus said to him, "Assuredly, I say to you that today, even this night, before the rooster **crows twice**,[17] you will deny Me three times."

b. First Denial, First Crow (Mark 14:68)

---

[17] According to *The NIV Study Bible*, "Some early manuscripts do not have twice."

Mark 14:66 Now as Peter was below in the courtyard, one of the servant girls of the high priest came.

Mark 14:67 And when she saw Peter warming himself, she looked at him and said, "You also were with Jesus of Nazareth."

Mark 14:68 But he denied it, saying, "I neither know nor understand what you are saying." And he went out on the porch, **and a rooster crowed**.[18]

c. Second Denial

Mark 14:69 And the servant girl saw him again, and began to say to those who stood by, "This is one of them."

Mark 14:70 But he denied it again. And a little later those who stood by said to Peter again, "Surely you are one of them; for you are a Galilean, and your speech shows it."

d. Third Denial, Second Crow (Mark 14:71-72)

Mark 14:71 Then he began to curse and swear, "I do not know this Man of whom you speak!"

Mark 14:72 **A second time**[19] the rooster crowed. Then Peter called to mind the word that Jesus had said to him, "Before the rooster crows twice, you will deny Me three times." And when he thought about it, he wept.

2. How Many Times did the Rooster Crow before Peter Denied Jesus Three Times?

Matthew	Mark	Luke	John
According to Matthew, the rooster would not crow	According to Mark, the rooster would crow <u>once</u>	According to Luke, the rooster would not crow	According to John, the rooster would not crow

---

[18] *The NIV Study Bible* does not include "and a rooster crowed." The text notes state: "Some early manuscripts *entryway* [porch] *and the rooster crowed.*"

[19] *The NIV Study Bible* text notes state: "Some early manuscripts do not have *the second time.*"

before Peter would deny Jesus three times and would crow <u>once</u> <u>thereafter</u>: Jesus said to Peter, "Assuredly, I say to you that <u>this</u> **night**, <u>before the</u> <u>rooster crows</u>, you will deny Me three times" (Mat 26:34).	before Peter would deny Jesus three times and <u>once</u> <u>thereafter</u>: Jesus said to Peter, "Assuredly, I say to you that **today**, <u>even</u> <u>this</u> **night,** <u>before the</u> <u>rooster crows</u> <u>twice</u>, you will deny Me three times" (Mark 14:30).	before Peter would deny Jesus three times and would crow <u>once</u> <u>thereafter</u>: Jesus said, "I tell you, Peter, the rooster <u>shall</u> <u>not crow this</u> **day** before you will deny three times that you know Me" (Luke 22:34).	before Peter would deny Jesus three times and would crow <u>once</u> <u>thereafter</u>: Jesus said to Peter, "Most assuredly, I say to you, the rooster <u>shall not</u> <u>crow</u> till you have denied Me three times" (John 13:38).

3. How Many Times Did Peter Deny Jesus before the Rooster Crowed?

Matthew	Mark	Luke	John
According to Matthew, Peter denied Jesus <u>three</u> <u>times</u> before the rooster crowed: Mat 26:69 ... a <u>servant girl</u> came to him, saying, "You also were with Jesus of Galilee." Mat 26:70 But he denied it	According to Mark, Peter denied Jesus <u>one time</u> before the rooster crowed and <u>twice</u> thereafter: First denial, first crow: <u>One of the</u> <u>servant girls</u> of the high priest saw Peter warming	According to Luke, Peter denied Jesus <u>three times</u> before the rooster crowed: Luke 22:56 ... a certain <u>servant girl</u>, seeing him as he sat by the fire, looked intently at him and said, "This man was also	According to John, Peter denied Jesus <u>three times</u> before the rooster crowed: John 18:17 Then the <u>servant girl</u> who kept the door said to Peter, "You are not also one of this Man's disciples, are

before them all …	himself and said, "You also were with Jesus of Nazareth" (Mark 14:67). He denied it, saying, "I neither know nor understand what you are saying." And he went out on the porch, and *a rooster crowed* (Mark 14:68).	with Him."	you?" He said, "I am not."
Mat 26:71 And when he had gone out to the gateway, another girl saw him and said to those who were there, "This fellow also was with Jesus of Nazareth."		Luke 22:57 But he denied Him …	…
		Luke 22:58 And after a little while another saw him and said, "You also are of them." But Peter said, "Man, I am not!"	John 18:25 … they said to him, "You are not also one of His disciples, are you?" He denied it …
Mat 26:72 But again he denied with an oath …			John 18:26 One of the servants of the high priest … said, "Did I not see you in the garden with Him?"
Mat 26:73 And a little later those who stood by came up and said to Peter, "Surely you also are one of them, for your speech betrays you."	Second denial: And the servant girl saw him again, and began to say to those who stood by, "This is one of them" (Mark 14:69). But he denied it again.	Luke 22:59 Then … another confidently affirmed, saying, "Surely this fellow also was with Him …"	
		Luke 22:60 But Peter said, "Man, I do not know what you are saying!" Immediately, while he was still speaking, the rooster crowed.	John 18:27 Peter then denied again; and immediately a rooster crowed.
Mat 26:74 Then he began to curse and swear, saying, "I do not know the	Third denial, second crow: And a little		

Man!" Immediately a rooster crowed.	later those who stood by said to Peter again, "Surely you are one of them ..." (Mark 14:70). Then he began to curse and swear, "I <u>do not know this Man</u> ...!" (Mark 14:71). A <u>second time the rooster crowed</u>. Then Peter called to mind the word that Jesus had said to him, "Before the rooster crows twice, you will deny Me three times" (Mark 14:72).		

III. ANALYSIS

There appears to be a contradiction between Mark 14:68, in which the rooster crows after Peter denies Jesus only once, and the following verses, in which Jesus says that Peter will deny Him three times before the rooster crows:

- Matthew 26:34: "Assuredly, I say to you that this night, before the rooster crows, you will deny Me three times."
- Luke 22:34: "I tell you, Peter, the rooster shall not crow this day before you will deny three times that you know Me."
- John 13:38: "Most assuredly, I say to you, the rooster shall not crow till you have denied Me three times."

According to Mark, the rooster crowed <u>once</u> before Peter denied Jesus three times, but according to Matthew, Luke and John, the rooster did not crow before Peter denied Jesus three times.

IV. POSSIBLE EXPLANATIONS

1. Explanation 1: The True Account is Mark and Other Books Give a Partial Account

a. Overview

Most likely, the full and accurate presentation of the story is from Mark, who is by tradition a disciple of Peter and would have thus known the story of Peter best.

Matthew, Luke and John likely did not leave in the detail that Peter would actually deny Jesus three times before the rooster would crow twice, as they may have contained a modified and simplified oral tradition. According to "How many times did the cock crow?"[20]:

Bear in mind that within this context, this is not considered "contradiction" or "error" -- no ancient reader would have thought this. Compromises in narrative presentation were often necessary to make a text more memorable for a population that was 90% illiterate. Intentional, structured

---

[20] Available at <http://www.tektonics.org/af/cockcrow.php>.

changes for a purpose are not, under such a semantic contract, an error.

Keener's Matthew commentary [635] adds a salient point: A cock's crowing lasted as long as five minutes and occurred at all hours; as Cicero wrote: "Is there any time, night or day, that cocks do not crow?" The "second" cockcrowing was usually associated with the dawn.

b. Problem with Explanation

This explanation is flawed because stating that the rooster would not crow before Peter denied Jesus three times is not a simplification of the statement that the rooster would not crow twice; it is a direct contradiction. If I were to state that a rooster would not crow before I said something three times, and the rooster crowed after I said it once, then my statement would be false. In other words, if Jesus really did state that "before the rooster crows, you will deny Me three times," as in Matthew 26:34, but the rooster in fact did crow before Peter denied him three times, as in Mark 14:68, then there would be a contradiction between Jesus' prediction in Matthew 26:34 and what actually occurred in Mark 14:68. In other words, if Jesus said that the rooster would not crow before Peter denied Jesus three times, but the rooster crowed after Peter denied Jesus just once, then Jesus' prediction would be incorrect.

In Mark, the rooster crowed after Peter denied Jesus only once, but in Matthew, Luke and John, the rooster crowed after Peter denied Jesus three times. Given this clear and plain contradiction, we cannot state that Matthew, Luke and Mark simply tried to simplify something complex for an illiterate audience. If they changed the text in Mark, then they would have altered the meaning. This, in turn, leaves one of two possible explanations:

- 1. The authors of the Gospels did not accurately record the words that were spoken and/or the events that transpired and, therefore, their accounts are unreliable; or
- 2. The authors of the Gospel accurately recorded the words that were spoken and the events that transpired, but later scribal errors resulted in contradictions between

the accounts of Matthew, Luke and John on the one hand and Mark on the other.

If either of these explanations is true, then we cannot rely on the Bible as fully infallible and perfectly preserved; either the authors erred in recording certain facts or later scribes failed to accurately transcribe the authors' texts.

2. Explanation 2: The Rooster Crowed Once but Scribes Mis-Transcribed the Mark Account

a. Overview

This explanation would account for why there are different translations of Mark 14:68, based on which English version of the Bible that is used, with some versions, such as the KJV, including the verse "and the cock crew," and the NIV, omitting this passage, thereby leaving only one account of a rooster crowing, in harmony with the accounts of Matthew, Luke and John.

b. Discrepant Versions

- Versions that State that the Cock Crowed in Mark 14:68

Version	Verse
ASV	Mark 14:68 But he denied, saying, I neither know, nor understand what thou sayest: and he went out into the porch; and the cock crew.
KJV	Mark 14:68 But he denied, saying, I know not, neither understand I what thou sayest. And he went out into the porch; and the cock crew.
NKJV	Mark 14:68 But he denied it, saying, "I neither know nor understand what you are saying." And he went out on the porch, and a rooster crowed.

- Versions that Do Not State that the Cock Crowed in Mark 14:68

Version	Verse

NIV	Mark 14:68 But he denied it. "I don't know or understand what you're talking about," he said, and went out into the entryway.
	[Footnote in the NIV: "Some early manuscripts *entryway and the rooster crowed.*]

c. Further Explanation

Omitting "and the rooster crowed" from Mark 14:68 in many ways solves the contradiction between Matthew, Luke and John, on the one hand, and Mark, on the other, because it leaves us with only one crowing of the rooster *after* Peter denied Jesus three times, as Jesus predicted. However, it still leaves us with the following problematic verses from Mark:

- Mark 14:30 Jesus said to him, "Assuredly, I say to you that today, even this night, before the <u>rooster crows twice</u>, you will deny Me three times."
- Mark 14:72 A <u>second time</u> the rooster crowed. Then Peter called to mind the word that Jesus had said to him, "Before the rooster <u>crows twice</u>, you will deny Me three times." And when he thought about it, he wept.

The NIV addresses this in the following footnotes:

- Footnote to Mark 14:30: "Some early manuscripts do not have *twice.*"
- Footnote to Mark 14:72: "Some early manuscripts do not have *the second time.* Some early manuscripts do not have *twice.*"

It is thus possible and likely that early manuscripts of Mark did not contain the reference to "twice" in Mark 14:30, did not contain the reference to "and the rooster crowed" in Mark 14:68 and did not contain the reference to "the second time" and "twice" in Mark 14:72, but these references were added in later manuscripts that were used for the KJV and other versions that relied on them, and the authentic accounts are actually those contained in Matthew, Luke and John, where Jesus stated that the rooster would not crow before Peter denied Jesus three times.

3. Explanation 3: "and the Rooster Crowed" in Mark 14:68 was a Scribal Addition

a. Overview

The third explanation is that the clause "and the rooster crowed," which is present in Mark 14:68 of the ASV, BBI, Darby, ESV, ISV, KJV, MKJV, NKJV, but not the NIV and RSV, was a scribal addition. This, in turn leaves two possibilities to reconcile the discrepant accounts:

b. The Rooster Crowed Twice in a Row After Peter Denied Jesus Three Times

Under this explanation, the rooster did not crow after the first denial in Mark 14:68 and the rooster crowed twice in a row after Peter denied Jesus three times. If this were the case, then there would be no contradiction between the accounts in Matthew, Luke and John, on the one hand, and Mark, on the other. Rather, Matthew, Luke and John would have given an account of the rooster crowing once and Mark would have given an account of the rooster crowing twice, but these would not be contradictions because if a rooster crows twice, it would also crow once, though Matthew, Luke and John would not have given an account of the second crowing. Provided the clause "and the rooster crowed" is removed from Mark 14:68, the contradiction would be resolved. If Matthew reports Jesus as saying "before the rooster crows, you will deny Me three times" (Mat 26:34) and Mark reports Jesus as saying "before the rooster crows twice, you will deny Me three times" (Mark 14:30), then we can conclude that the rooster crowed twice in a row after Peter denied Jesus three times, that Mark gives the more detailed account and that Matthew, Luke and John give a simplified version without the added detail "twice."

c. The Rooster Crowed Once, but "Twice" was Inserted into Mark 14:30 and Mark 14:72 by Scribes

Under this explanation, the rooster crowed only once after Peter denied Jesus three times. The reference to the crow of the rooster in Mark 14:68 was a scribal addition, as was the addition of the word "twice" in Mark 14:30 and Mark 14:72. Under this explanation, all three references to two crows in the Mark account are due to scribal additions.

4. Explanation 4: The Cock Crowing Refers to the Crow at Dawn

a. Overview

The discrepancy can be resolved if the cock crowing in Matthew, Luke and John refers to the crow at dawn. According to this explanation, when people refer to the cock crow they generally mean the crow that happens closer to dawn. In reality, however, cocks also crow in the middle of the night. Without any further clarification, it can be assumed that the dawn crowing was intended by Matthew, Luke and John. However, Mark provides the extra detail showing that Peter denied Jesus three times before the dawn crowing, but in addition to this, the rooster crowed once after Peter's first denial but before his second denial, and then again once before his third denial.[21]

b. Explanation Provided by *Fausset's Bible Dictionary*

a. *Overview*

This explanation assumes that by "crow," Jesus meant the crow of the rooster at dawn. *Fausset's Bible Dictionary* provides textual evidence to support this reading. Under the definition of "Crow," Fausset provides as follows:

> "Cockcrowing" was the third watch of the four watches introduced by the Romans. (See WATCHES) The Jews originally had but three. The first ended at 9, the second at 12, the third or "cockcrowing" at 3, and the <u>fourth at 6 o'clock a.m.</u> (Mark 13:35). The second cockcrowing (Mark 14:72), which marked Peter's third denial of Jesus, was probably at

---

[21] This explanation is advanced by Apologetics Press. See
<https://www.apologeticspress.org/apcontent.aspx?category=6&article=759
>.

the beginning of the <u>fourth watch between 3 and 4</u> in the morning not long before the first day dawn, just when our Lord was being led bound to Caiaphas across the court where Peter was standing. The Mishna [known as the "Oral Torah," it is the first major written collection of the Jewish oral traditions and is the first major work of Rabbinic literature] states that "cocks were not bred at Jerusalem because of the holy things. "But Peter could easily hear their shrill crow on mount Olivet, only a half mile off from where he was on the porch of the high priest's palace, in the stillness of night. Moreover, the restriction could only apply to the Jews, not to the Romans who used fowl for food. The first crowing being fainter in the distance did not awaken his slumbering conscience; but the second with its loud sound was the crowing which alone is recorded by Matthew (Mat 26:34), Luke (Luk 22:34), and John (Joh 13:38), being that which roused him to remember bitterly his Lord's neglected warning.

b.   *The Watches*

- First watch: ended at 9
- Second watch: ended at 12
- Third or "cockcrowing" watch: ended at 3:00 am
- Fourth watch: started between 3:00 am to 4:00 am; ended at 6:00 am (Mark 13:35). The second crowing was probably at the beginning of the <u>fourth watch between 3 and 4</u> in the morning not long before the first day dawn, just when our Lord was being led bound to Caiaphas across the court where Peter was standing.

c. Problem with This Explanation: Jesus Said Peter would Deny Him "This Night"

A problem with this explanation is that Jesus said Peter would deny Him "this night" before the rooster crows, not "tomorrow near dawn." According to Matthew and Mark:

- Jesus said to Peter, "Assuredly, I say to you that <u>this night</u>, <u>before the rooster crows</u>, you will deny Me three times" (Mat 26:34).

- Jesus said to Peter, "Assuredly, I say to you that today, <u>even this night, before the rooster crows twice</u>, you will deny Me three times" (Mark 14:30).

Luke and John do not include the added detail of "this night." Luke states "this day" and John is silent as to the timing. We should derive from this that the denials would occur that evening, and before the next day, since Jesus was speaking to Peter at the last supper and so the only way for the denials to have occurred "this day" would have had to also have been "this night." Therefore, the three denials would have had to have taken place that night.

Matthew states that just after Peter denied Jesus the third time, the rooster crowed: "Then he began to curse and swear, saying, 'I do not know the Man!' Immediately a rooster crowed" (Mat 26:74). Luke and John also state that the rooster crowed immediately after the third denial (Luke 22:60; John 18:27). Therefore, if Peter had denied Jesus three times that night, and the rooster crowed immediately thereafter, then the rooster must have crowed that evening, before the dawn crowing of the rooster. Therefore, the proposed explanation of the crow of the rooster referring to the dawn crow cannot be accurate. Rather, the crow must be referring to whatever crow could be expected to take place next, therefore creating a contradiction between Matthew, Luke and John, where the rooster crowed after Peter denied Jesus three times, and Mark, where the rooster crowed after Peter denied Jesus the first time.

d. Reply to the Problem

It is possible that by "this night," Jesus meant that Peter would deny Jesus at some point in the evening and the early morning of the next day, before dawn. If the crow was a reference to the crow at the beginning of the fourth watch between 3 and 4 in the morning not long before the first day dawn, then Peter's third denial would have occurred immediately before this crow. The three denials would have all fallen within the limits and definition of "this night," if "night" is taken to mean the evening before dawn.

It is important not to interpose a western lens when reading Jesus' reference to "this night" in Matthew and Mark and "today" and "this day" in Luke. Read with a western lens, it would seem Jesus meant Peter would deny him three times before the evening of that day, which would have ended at 12:00 am. However, we must look at the words within the Jewish context in which they were spoken. The Jewish day starts at nightfall, and continues throughout the night and following day, until the next night. Therefore, when Jesus said "this night," he was refers to the night of "this day," which did not end at midnight. Rather, it went all the way until nightfall of the next day. Therefore, the night would have ended at dawn, not at 12:00 am. The prediction was that Peter would have denied Jesus three times by the time the rooster crowed at dawn, which he did.

CHAPTER 22. ONE GOD OR MANY?
POLYTHESISM IN THE BIBLE

I. POLYTHEISM SUGGESTED IN PSALMS

Psa 82:1 God stands in the congregation of the mighty; He judges among the gods.

Psa 82:6 I said, "You are gods, And all of you are children of the Most High.

Psa 82:7 But you shall die like men, And fall like one of the princes."

II. EXPLANATION

This appears to support the idea of polytheism. However, according to the NIV study Bible note at Psa 82:1, "In the language of the OT—and in accordance with the conceptual world of the ancient Near East—rulers and judges, as deputies of the heavenly King, could be given the honorific title 'god'" or be called "son of God." The fact that these "gods" were not meant to be like God in a literal sense is attested to by the fact that they "will come to death like men, falling like one of the rulers of the earth" (Psa 82:7).

CHAPTER 23. THE TEN COMMANDMENTS (EXO 20 AND DEU 5)

Maurice Bucaille claims:

"There is good reason to believe that after the Jewish people settled in Canaan, at the end of the Thirteenth century B.C., writing was used to preserve and hand down the tradition. There was not however complete accuracy, even in what to men seems to demand the greatest durability, i.e. the laws. Among these, the laws which are supposed to have been written by God's own hand, the Ten Commandments, were transmitted in the Old Testament in two versions; Exodus (20,1-21) and Deuteronomy (5, 1-30). They are the same in spirit, but the variations are obvious."

These variations do not however undermine the validity or accuracy of the text. Rather, where the accounts of God's words are not identical, the author gives account of some additional words that God also spoke that the other author does not mention. But these are not contradictions. Rather, when Moses gave account of God's words in Deuteronomy, he includes an extra sentence and omits another here and there. However, where the matter is the same, the language is identical, which speaks to the accuracy of the account.

For example, suppose God said:

'Observe the Sabbath day, to keep it holy, as the LORD your God commanded you.
Six days you shall labor and do all your work,
but the seventh day is the Sabbath of the LORD your God. In it you shall do no work: you, nor your son, nor your daughter, nor your male servant, nor your female servant, nor your ox, nor your donkey, nor any of your cattle, nor your stranger who is within your gates, that your male servant and your female servant may rest as well as you.

For in six days the LORD made the heavens and the earth, the sea, and all that is in them, and rested the seventh day. Therefore the LORD blessed the Sabbath day and hallowed it.

And remember that you were a slave in the land of Egypt, and the LORD your God brought you out from there by a mighty hand and by an outstretched arm; therefore the LORD your God commanded you to keep the Sabbath day.

First, we should recognize that the original Hebrew texts did not have quotation marks. They are thus not meant to give God's exact word for word commandments; they are meant to capture the ideas.

Therefore, because no claim is made that God spoke these exact words or *only* these words, it would not be inaccurate for the author of Exodus 20 to give an account of all of these words, in their exactitude, but to omit only "nor your ox, nor your donkey" and "For in six days the LORD made the heavens and the earth, the sea, and all that is in them, and rested the seventh day. Therefore the LORD blessed the Sabbath day and hallowed it," unless the author was claiming that God spoke *only* these words. If the author stated that God spoke *only* these words, then there would be a contradiction with Deuteronomy 5, which states that God also spoke the words, "nor your ox, nor your donkey" and "For in six days the LORD made the heavens and the earth, the sea, and all that is in them, and rested the seventh day. Therefore the LORD blessed the Sabbath day and hallowed it." Yet because the author never makes such a claim, there is no contradiction. Similarly, because the author of Deuteronomy 5 never makes the claim that God spoke *only* the words reported therein, there is no contradiction there either.

Exodus 20	Deuteronomy 5
Exo 20:8 "Remember the Sabbath day, to keep it holy.	Deu 5:12 'Observe the Sabbath day, to keep it holy, as the LORD your God commanded you.
Exo 20:9 Six days you shall labor and do all your work,	Deu 5:13 Six days you shall labor and do all your work,

Exo 20:10 but the seventh day is the Sabbath of the LORD your God. In it you shall do no work: you, nor your son, nor your daughter, nor your male servant, nor your female servant, nor your cattle, nor your stranger who is within your gates.	Deu 5:14 but the seventh day is the Sabbath of the LORD your God. In it you shall do no work: you, nor your son, nor your daughter, nor your male servant, nor your female servant, nor *your ox, nor your donkey, nor any of* your cattle, nor your stranger who is within your gates, *that your male servant and your female servant may rest as well as you.*
Exo 20:11 *For in six days the LORD made the heavens and the earth, the sea, and all that is in them, and rested the seventh day. Therefore the LORD blessed the Sabbath day and hallowed it.*	Deu 5:15 *And remember that you were a slave in the land of Egypt, and the LORD your God brought you out from there by a mighty hand and by an outstretched arm; therefore the LORD your God commanded you to keep the Sabbath day.*

This is a full account of Exodus 20 and Deuteronomy 5, with the variations among them in bold italics:

Exodus 20	Deuteronomy 5
Exo 20:1 And God spoke all these words, saying:	Deu 5:5 I stood between the LORD and you at that time, to declare to you the word of the LORD; for you were afraid because of the fire, and you did not go up the mountain. He said:
Exo 20:2 "I am the LORD your God, who brought you	Deu 5:6 'I am the LORD your God who brought you out of the land of Egypt, out of the

out of the land of Egypt, out of the house of bondage.	house of bondage.
Exo 20:3 "You shall have no other gods before Me.	Deu 5:7 'You shall have no other gods before Me.
Exo 20:4 "You shall not make for yourself a carved image—any likeness of anything that is in heaven above, or that is in the earth beneath, or that is in the water under the earth;	Deu 5:8 'You shall not make for yourself a carved image—any likeness of anything that is in heaven above, or that is in the earth beneath, or that is in the water under the earth;
Exo 20:5 you shall not bow down to them nor serve them. For I, the LORD your God, am a jealous God, visiting the iniquity of the fathers upon the children to the third and fourth generations of those who hate Me,	Deu 5:9 you shall not bow down to them nor serve them. For I, the LORD your God, am a jealous God, visiting the iniquity of the fathers upon the children to the third and fourth generations of those who hate Me,
Exo 20:6 but showing mercy to thousands, to those who love Me and keep My commandments.	Deu 5:10 but showing mercy to thousands, to those who love Me and keep My commandments.
Exo 20:7 "You shall not take the name of the LORD your God in vain, for the LORD will not hold him guiltless who takes His name in vain.	Deu 5:11 'You shall not take the name of the LORD your God in vain, for the LORD will not hold him guiltless who takes His name in vain.
Exo 20:8 "Remember the Sabbath day, to keep it holy.	Deu 5:12 'Observe the Sabbath day, to keep it holy, *as the LORD your God commanded you.*
Exo 20:9 Six days you shall labor and do all your work,	Deu 5:13 Six days you shall labor and do all your work,
Exo 20:10 but the seventh	Deu 5:14 but the seventh

day is the Sabbath of the LORD your God. In it you shall do no work: you, nor your son, nor your daughter, nor your male servant, nor your female servant, nor your cattle, nor your stranger who is within your gates.	day is the Sabbath of the LORD your God. In it you shall do no work: you, nor your son, nor your daughter, nor your male servant, nor your female servant, nor your ox, nor your donkey, nor any of your cattle, nor your stranger who is within your gates, that your male servant and your female servant may rest as well as you.
Exo 20:11 *For in six days the LORD made the heavens and the earth, the sea, and all that is in them, and rested the seventh day. Therefore the LORD blessed the Sabbath day and hallowed it.*	Deu 5:15 *And remember that you were a slave in the land of Egypt, and the LORD your God brought you out from there by a mighty hand and by an outstretched arm; therefore the LORD your God commanded you to keep the Sabbath day.*
Exo 20:12 "Honor your father and your mother, that your days may be long upon the land which the LORD your God is giving you.	Deu 5:16 'Honor your father and your mother, as the LORD your God has commanded you, that your days may be long, and that it may be well with you in the land which the LORD your God is giving you.
Exo 20:13 "You shall not murder.	Deu 5:17 'You shall not murder.
Exo 20:14 "You shall not commit adultery.	Deu 5:18 'You shall not commit adultery.
Exo 20:15 "You shall not steal.	Deu 5:19 'You shall not steal.
Exo 20:16 "You shall not bear false witness against your	Deu 5:20 'You shall not bear false witness against your

neighbor.	neighbor.
Exo 20:17 "You shall not covet your neighbor's house; you shall not covet your neighbor's wife, nor his male servant, nor his female servant, nor his ox, nor his donkey, nor anything that is your neighbor's."	Deu 5:21 'You shall not covet your neighbor's wife; and you shall not desire your neighbor's house, his field, his male servant, his female servant, his ox, his donkey, or anything that is your neighbor's.'
Exo 20:18 Now all the people witnessed the thunderings, the lightning flashes, the sound of the trumpet, and the mountain smoking; and when the people saw it, they trembled and stood afar off.	Deu 5:22 "These words the LORD spoke to all your assembly, in the mountain from the midst of the fire, the cloud, and the thick darkness, with a loud voice; and *He added no more*. And He wrote them on two tablets of stone and gave them to me.

However, to Maurice Bucaille's credit, I will concede that although in Deu 5:22, it states that God "added no more" to the words spoken therein, Exodus 20 contains words not contained in Deuteronomy 5. There thus appears to be a contradiction between the two. And this cannot be explained by the fact that Moses broke the commandments and God rewrote them, as explained in Exodus 32 and 34, respectively, because the second time, God said "I will write on these tablets the words that were on the first tablets which you broke" (Exo 34:1).

CHAPTER 24. WAS JESUS' ROBE SCARLET OR PURPLE?

I. CONTRADICTORY VERSES

- The soldiers took Jesus into the Praetorium hall, gathered the whole garrison around Him (Mat 27:27), stripped Him and put a <u>scarlet</u> [brilliant red] robe on Him (Mat 27:28).
- Then the soldiers led Him to Praetorium hall, called together the whole garrison (Mark 15:16) and clothed Him with <u>purple</u> (Mark 15:17).
- The soldiers twisted a crown of thorns and on His head and put on Him a purple robe (John 19:2).

II. EXPLANATION

People often see colors differently. Some colorblind people even have difficulty distinguishing between certain colors, such as red and green or blue and purple. Yet even those who can distinguish between some colors may be more specific as to color naming. For example, what one person calls red another person may call scarlet.

Architects and interior designers recognize that colors cannot be accurately described by words. For this reason, as a rule of thumb, they order samples of products in order to see for themselves exactly the color that is being sold and purchased. The reason for this is that what one person may call one color may mean something entirely different for another person.

Matthew, Mark and Luke each wrote different accounts of the life of Jesus. Mark based much of his account on the preaching of Peter, and eyewitness. Matthew and John were both eyewitnesses. What they all had in common was that they either saw the robe themselves or based their account on others who saw it.

It is natural in such a scenario for the reporting of the exact color of the robe to come across differently, particularly when purple and scarlet are closely-related colors, both based on red. Scarlet is a deep, dark red. It is far from bright or orange in tone. Purple is a mixture of blue and red. It is possible that the robe was scarlet with a bluish tint and slightly faded, such that what John saw as scarlet was described by Matthew and Mark generically as purple, while John used the more exact term scarlet.

Moreover, in the first century, there were several shades of purple and scarlet that were difficult to distinguish from one another. The ancient Romans used the term purple when speaking of various shades of red (J.W. McGarvey, Commentary on Matthew and Mark (1875, Delight AR: Gospel Light, p. 361; Albert Barnes, Barnes' Notes (Electronic Database: e-Sword).

CHAPTER 25. WAS KORAH ELIPHAZ'S BROTHER OR SON? (GEN 36)

According to Gen 36:5, Korah was Esau's son through Oholibamah (Gen 36:5).

This would make Korah Eliphaz's brother, since Eliphaz was also Esau's son, through Adah (Gen 36:4).

Under Gen 36:11, the sons of Eliphaz were Teman, Omar, Zepho, Gatam and Kenaz.

However, according to Gen 36:16, Korah was one of Eliphaz's sons (Gen 36:15). This contradicts both Gen 36:5 and Gen 36:11, which when read together would have Korah as Eliphaz's brother, not as his son.

This could be understood by explaining the reference to "son" in Gen 36:5 as really referencing "grandson" (*i.e.*, stating that Korah was Esau's descendant through another son—in this case, Eliphaz). However, that would not be possible, since Gen 36:14 specifically states that Oholibamah bore Korah "to Esau" (Gen 36:14), not to Esau's son Eliphaz (*i.e.*, through an act of incest).

The NIV Study Bible notes that Korah only appears as a son of Eliphaz in the Masoretic Text and is omitted from the Samaritan Pentateuch.

CHAPTER 26. WHO CARRIED JESUS' CROSS: JESUS OR SIMON?

I. OVERVIEW

The Gospel accounts vary regarding who carried the cross on which Jesus was crucified. In Matthew, Mark and Luke, it was Simon of Cyrene; in John, it was Jesus.

> Mat 27:31 And when they had mocked Him, they took the robe off Him, put His own clothes on Him, and led Him away to be crucified. Mat 27:32 Now as they came out, they found a man of Cyrene, <u>Simon</u> by name. Him they <u>compelled to bear His cross</u>.
>
> Mark 15:20 And when they had mocked Him, they took the purple off Him, put His own clothes on Him, and led Him out to crucify Him. Mark 15:21 Then they compelled a certain man, <u>Simon a Cyrenian</u>, the father of Alexander and Rufus, as he was coming out of the country and passing by, <u>to bear His cross</u>.
>
> Luke 23:25 And he released to them the one they requested, who for rebellion and murder had been thrown into prison; but he delivered Jesus to their will. Luke 23:26 Now as they led Him away, they laid hold of a certain man, <u>Simon a Cyrenian</u>, who was coming from the country, and <u>on him they laid the cross</u> that he might bear it after Jesus.
>
> John 19:16 Then he delivered Him to them to be crucified. Then they took Jesus and led Him away. John 19:17 And <u>He, bearing His cross</u>, went out to a place called the Place of a Skull, which is called in Hebrew, Golgotha.

Matthew	Mark	Luke	John
Mat 27:31 And when	Mark 15:20 And when	Luke 23:25 And he	John 19:16 Then he

they had mocked Him, they took the robe off Him, put His own clothes on Him,	they had mocked Him, they took the purple off Him, put His own clothes on Him,	released to them the one they requested, who for rebellion and murder had been thrown into prison; but he delivered Jesus to their will.	delivered Him to them to be crucified.
and <u>led Him away</u> to be crucified.	and <u>led Him out</u> to crucify Him.	Luke 23:26 Now as they <u>led Him away</u>,	Then they took Jesus and <u>led Him away</u>.
Mat 27:32 Now as they came out, they found a man of Cyrene, Simon by name.	Mark 15:21 Then they compelled a certain man, Simon a Cyrenian, the father of Alexander and Rufus,	they laid hold of a certain man, Simon a Cyrenian,	John 19:17 And <u>He, bearing His cross</u>, went out to a place called the Place of a Skull, which is called in Hebrew, Golgotha.
	as he was coming out of the country and passing by,	who was coming from the country,	
Him they compelled to bear His	to bear His cross.	and on him they laid the cross that he might bear it	

cross.		after Jesus.	

II. EXPLANATION

The traditional explanation is that both Jesus and Simon of Cyrene carried the cross. Matthew, Mark and Luke do not state that only Simon carried the cross; nor does John state that only Jesus carried the cross. John 19:17 simply states that Jesus bore his cross. Most likely, Jesus set off from the place of his conviction with the crossbeam on his shoulders. When he reached the city gates, he collapsed under the weight of the cross, following the physical trauma his body had experienced. At that point, the Roman soldiers ordered Simon to carry the cross beam.

1. Attempted Harmonization

a. Overview

In Matthew 27:31, we read that after the soldiers mocked Jesus and "took the robe off Him [and] put His own clothes on Him," they "led Him away to be crucified." Most likely, as they led him away to be crucified, they forced him to bear the crossbeam of his cross. Matthew 27:32 then states that "as they came out, they found a man of Cyrene, Simon by name." Most likely, Matthew is referring to the soldier's exit from the city walls towards Golgotha. At that point, Matthew 27:32 states that the soldiers "compelled" Simon "to bear" Jesus' cross. Most likely, Jesus bore the cross from the place of his conviction to the city walls, at which point carrying the cross was shifted to Simon.

b. Line-by-Line Account

a. *Mark*

Matthew states:

Mat 27:31 And when they had mocked Him, they took the robe off Him, put His own clothes on Him, and led Him away to be crucified.

These actions commenced in the city of Jerusalem, where Jesus was condemned.

> Mat 27:32 Now as they came out, they found a man of Cyrene, Simon by name. Him they compelled to bear His cross.

Then, as they "came out" of the city of Jerusalem, the soldiers compelled Simon of Cyrene to bear Jesus' cross, presumably because Jesus', in a weakened and traumatized physical state, was unable to bear the weight of the cross all the way to Golgotha.

b.   Mark and Luke

Mark's and Luke's account agrees with Matthew's account, but they add one further detail: The soldiers ordered Simon to carry Jesus' cross as Simon was coming out of the country and passing by. Mark states "as he was coming out of the country and passing by" (Mark 15:21) and Luke states, "who was coming from the country" (Luke 23:26). This would be consistent with the view that Simon was compelled to bear Jesus' cross after Jesus reached Jerusalem's city walls and set out for Golgotha. After Jesus reached the city walls and into the country towards Golgotha, Simon was recruited to carry the cross.

c.   John

John's account states:

John 19:16 Then he delivered Him to them to be crucified. Then they took Jesus and <u>led Him away</u>.
John 19:17 And He, <u>bearing His cross,</u> <u>went out to a place called the Place of a Skull,</u> which is called in Hebrew, Golgotha.

If the soldiers intercepted Simon in the country as he was passing by and had him bear the cross from the country (i.e., outside of the city gates) to Golgotha, then the account in John must be referring to Jesus' bearing the cross from the place of conviction in Jerusalem to the city walls.

2. Why Didn't Jesus Bear the Cross All the Way to Golgotha: Physical Trauma Jesus Bore

The physical trauma that Jesus underwent prior to being ordered to carry his cross in John 19:17 is recorded as follows:

- Luke 22:44 And being in agony, He prayed more earnestly. Then His sweat became like great drops of blood falling down to the ground.
- John 18:22 And when He had said these things, one of the officers who stood by struck Jesus with the palm of his hand, saying, "Do You answer the high priest like that?" John 18:23 Jesus answered him, "If I have spoken evil, bear witness of the evil; but if well, why do you strike Me?"
- Mark 14:65 Then some began to spit on Him, and to blindfold Him, and to beat Him, and to say to Him, "Prophesy!" And the officers struck Him with the palms of their hands.
- Mat 27:26 Then he released Barabbas to them; and when he had scourged Jesus, he delivered Him to be crucified.
- Mat 27:29 When they had twisted a crown of thorns, they put it on His head, and a reed in His right hand. And they bowed the knee before Him and mocked Him, saying, "Hail, King of the Jews!" Mat 27:30 Then they spat on Him, and took the reed and struck Him on the head. Mat 27:31 And when they had mocked Him, they took the robe off Him, put His own clothes on Him, and led Him away to be crucified.

Jesus started to carry the cross, but He simply could not bear it very far after all the physical trauma He bore. He collapsed. That is when the Romans drafted Simon of Cyrene to carry the cross the rest of the way.[22]

---

[22] Taken from https://carm.org/bible-difficulties/matthew-mark/did-jesus-or-simon-cyrene-carry-cross.

3. Why Do Matthew, Mark and Luke, on the One Hand, and John, on the Other, Offer Discrepant Accounts of Who Bore the Cross?

The population of Jerusalem during Passover would have swelled to a number higher than any normal week. Thus, it would have been virtually impossible for Matthew or John to follow Jesus every step of the way from conviction to crucifixion. Matthew recorded Roman officials ordering Simon the Cyrene to carry the crossbeam from outside the gates to Golgotha from his vantage point, whereas John recorded Jesus carrying the crossbeam through the city streets, from his own vantage point. It is possible that both Matthew and John were unable to follow Jesus the entire journey to Golgotha, and so each recorded only what he saw.[23]

This explanation would be consistent with the likelihood that John, one of the inner three of Jesus' apostles, would have been present at the time and place of Jesus' conviction.

4. Bible Commentaries

a.   Albert Barnes' Notes on the Bible

Albert Barnes' Notes on the Bible makes this point. It states:

> John says that Jesus went forth "bearing his cross." Luke says Luk_23:26 that they laid the cross on Simon, that he might bear it after Jesus. There is no contradiction in these accounts. It was a part of the usual punishment of those who were crucified that they should bear their own cross to the place of execution. Accordingly, it was laid at first on Jesus, and he went forth, as John says, bearing it. Weak, however, and exhausted by suffering and watchfulness, he probably sunk under the heavy burden, and they laid hold of Simon that he might bear "one end" of the cross, as Luke says, "after Jesus." The cross was composed of two pieces of wood, one of which was placed upright in the earth, and the other crossed it after the form of the figure of a cross. The upright

---

[23] See <https://answersingenesis.org/contradictions-in-the-bible/who-really-carried-the-cross-of-jesus/>.

part was commonly so high that the feet of the person crucified were 2 or 3 feet from the ground.

b. Adam Clarke's Commentary on the Bible

Adam Clarke's Commentary on the Bible states:

In John, we are told Christ himself bore the cross, and this, it is likely, he did for a part of the way; but, being exhausted with the scourging and other cruel usage which he had received, he was found incapable of bearing it alone; therefore they obliged Simon, not, I think, to bear it entirely, but to assist Christ, by bearing a part of it. It was a constant practice among the Romans, to oblige criminal to bear their cross to the place of execution: insomuch that Plutarch makes use of it as an illustration of the misery of vice. "Every kind of wickedness produces its own particular torment, just as every malefactor, when he is brought forth to execution, carries his own cross." See Lardner's Credib. vol. i. p. 160.

c. The NIV Study Bible

The NIV Study Bible note at Mark 15:21 states:

Men condemned to death were usually forced to carry a beam of the cross, often weighing 30 or 40 pounds, to the place of the crucifixion. Jesus started out by carrying his (see Jn 19:17), but he had been so weakened by flogging that Simon was pressed into service.

The NIV Study Bible note at John 19:17 further states:

Somewhere along the way Simon of Cyrene took Jesus' cross (Mk 15:21), probably because Jesus was weakened by the flogging.

CHAPTER 27. WHO JUDGES THE WORLD, GOD THE FATHER OR JESUS?

I. OVERVIEW

Who is it who judges?

- In John 5, Jesus states that the Father judges no one and Jesus judges;
- in John 12, Jesus states that he does not judge anyone who does not believe and that the "word" judges he who rejects Jesus;
- 1 Peter 1 states that the Father judges according to each one's work;
- 1 Corinthians 6 states that the saints will judge the world.

First, the Bible states that Jesus judges and the Father does not judge; then it states that Jesus does not judge and the "word" judges; then it states that the Father judges; then it states that the saints judge. It thus seems undisputed that the word and the saints judge, but whether Jesus or the Father judges depends on which verse of the Bible one relies upon.

II. RELEVANT VERSES

1. John 5 and 2 Timothy 4 State that the Father Judges No One; All Judgment Has Been Committed to Jesus

Several verses of the Bible state that Jesus is charged with judging mankind. John 5 makes clear that the Father has granted the Son authority to judge. John states:

John 5:21 For as the Father raises the dead and gives life to them, even so the Son gives life to whom He will.

John 5:22 For *the Father judges no one*, but *has committed all judgment to the Son*,
John 5:23 that all should honor the Son just as they honor the Father. He who does not honor the Son does not honor the Father who sent Him.
…
John 5:26 For as the Father has life in Himself, so He has granted the Son to have life in Himself,
John 5:27 and *has given Him authority to execute judgment* also, because He is the Son of Man.
John 5:28 Do not marvel at this; for the hour is coming in which all who are in the graves will hear His voice
John 5:29 and come forth—those who have done good, to the resurrection of life, and those who have done evil, to the resurrection of condemnation.

Jesus' judgment is based on the Father's will, but the Father has delegated to Jesus the authority to judge:

John 5:30 I can of Myself do nothing. *As I hear, I judge*; and My judgment is righteous, because I do not seek My own will but the will of the Father who sent Me.
John 5:31 "If I bear witness of Myself, My witness is not true.

2 Timothy also states that Jesus will judge the living and the dead "at His appearing":

2Ti 4:1 I charge you therefore before God and the Lord Jesus Christ, who will judge the living and the dead at His appearing and His kingdom.

2. John 12 States that Jesus Does not Judge Anyone Who Does Not Believe, but the Word Judges He Who Rejects Jesus

However, in John 12, Jesus states that he does not judge anyone who does not believe and that the "word" judges he who rejects Jesus:

John 12:47 And if anyone hears My words and does not believe, *I do not judge him; for I did not come to judge the world* but to save the world.

John 12:48 He who rejects Me, and does not receive My words, has that which judges him—*the word that I have spoken will judge him in the last day*.
John 12:49 For *I have not spoken on My own authority*; but the Father who sent Me *gave Me a command, what I should say and what I should speak*.
John 12:50 And I know that His command is everlasting life. Therefore, whatever I speak, just as the Father has told Me, so I speak."

3. 1 Peter 1 States that the Father Judges

1 Peter 1 states that the Father judges according to each one's work:

1Pe 1:17 And if you call on the Father, *who without partiality judges according to each one's work*, conduct yourselves throughout the time of your stay here in fear;
1Pe 1:18 knowing that you were not redeemed with corruptible things, like silver or gold, from your aimless conduct received by tradition from your fathers,
1Pe 1:19 but with the precious blood of Christ, as of a lamb without blemish and without spot.

4. 1 Corinthians 6 States that the Saints Judge

1 Corinthians 6 states that the saints will judge the world:

1Co 6:2 Do you not know that *the saints will judge the world*? And if the world will be judged by you, are you unworthy to judge the smallest matters?
1Co 6:3 Do you not know that we shall judge angels? How much more, things that pertain to this life?
1Co 6:4 If then you have judgments concerning things pertaining to this life, do you appoint those who are least esteemed by the church to judge?

5. Matthew 19 States that the Disciples Will Judge the Twelve Tribes

Matthew 19 states that the disciples will judge the twelve tribes of Israel:

Mat 19:27 Then Peter answered and said to Him, "See, we have left all and followed You. Therefore what shall we have?"

Mat 19:28 So Jesus said to them, "Assuredly I say to you, that in the regeneration, when the Son of Man sits on the throne of His glory, you who have followed Me will also sit on twelve thrones, judging the twelve tribes of Israel.

III. EXPLANATIONS

1. Introduction

The apparent contradiction in the verses can be reconciled by two explanations:

- Jesus did not judge in the earthly ministry of his first coming, but will judge in his second coming. Therefore, Jesus both judges (in his second coming) and does not judge (in his first coming);
- The Father judges through Jesus, whereas Jesus judges as the Father's agent. Therefore, the Father both judges (indirectly, through Jesus) and does not judge (directly).

These are *not* meant to be explanations in the alternative. Rather, they are intended as symbiotic explanations that apply simultaneously.

2. Explanation 1: Jesus Did Not Judge in the Earthly Ministry of His First Coming, But Will Judge in His Second Coming

John 5 states that the Father has granted the Son authority to judge, but in John 12, Jesus states that he does not judge anyone who does not believe and that the "word" judges he who rejects Jesus. It thus appears that, on the one hand, Jesus judges, but on the other, Jesus does not judge anyone who does not believe. How can this be reconciled? It would appear that Jesus has been granted all authority to judge, but he does not judge He who does not believe. This apparent discrepancy can be explained as a matter of time. It might be that John 5 is referring to Jesus' authority to judge on the last day, whereas John 12 is referring to Jesus' holding back of judgment during his earthly ministry.

John 5 might thus be referring to Jesus when He returns, while John 12 is referring to Jesus' ministry as God incarnate, who came to offer salvation to the world.

While Jesus walked the earth as a man, He did not judge sinners. Rather, He exercised the forgiveness of sins. Many examples abound:

- In John 8, the scribes and Pharisees brought to Jesus a woman caught in adultery and asked Jesus whether she should be stoned. Jesus said to them, "He who is without sin among you, let him throw a stone at her first" (John 8:7). The woman's accusers then departed. Jesus then told the woman that He does not condemn her and to "go and sin no more" (John 8:11).
- In John 4, when Jesus sat at Jacob's well, a Samaritan woman came to draw water. Jesus said to her, "Give Me a drink" (John 4:7). He told the woman "you have had five husbands, and the one whom you now have is not your husband" (John 4:18) but he never judged her.

Jesus states that the Father "has given Him authority to execute judgment also, because He is the Son of Man. Do not marvel at this; for the hour is coming in which all who are in the graves will hear His voice and come forth—those who have done good, to the resurrection of life, and those who have done evil, to the resurrection of condemnation" (John 5:27-29). It thus would appear that Jesus is given authority to judge on judgment day, but this authority is different from the role He was to play in His earthly ministry, during which He offered forgiveness for sins rather than judgment. It can thus be stated that all judgment has been committed to Jesus to judge in the last day, and yet Jesus does not judge anyone who does not believe.

That Jesus will return to the earth as judge at his second coming is made evident by Matthew 25:

Mat 25:31 "When the Son of Man comes in His glory, and all the holy angels with Him, then He will sit on the throne of His glory.

Mat 25:32 All the nations will be gathered before Him, and He will separate them one from another, as a shepherd divides his sheep from the goats.

Mat 25:33 And He will set the sheep on His right hand, but the goats on the left.

Mat 25:34 Then the King will say to those on His right hand, 'Come, you blessed of My Father, inherit the kingdom prepared for you from the foundation of the world:

Mat 25:35 for I was hungry and you gave Me food; I was thirsty and you gave Me drink; I was a stranger and you took Me in;

Mat 25:36 I was naked and you clothed Me; I was sick and you visited Me; I was in prison and you came to Me.'

3. Explanation 2: Jesus Judges as the Father's Agent

The verses could potentially by reconciled by giving attention to Acts 17:31, which states that God "has appointed a day on which He will judge the world in righteousness by the Man whom He has ordained. He has given assurance of this to all by raising Him from the dead." This indicates that Jesus judges as an agent of God. On this basis, we can conclude that one possible interpretation of John 12 is that when Jesus states that He "did not come to judge the world," He does not literally mean that He does not judge. Rather, He is stating that His judgment is not His own, but is the judgment of His word, which Jesus has received from the Father. In other words, Jesus' judgment is the Father's. Therefore, the Father does not judge directly, but has entrusted all judgment to the Son, who judges on the Father's behalf through the word. In other words, the Father is judging, but through the word, which He has given to Jesus.

When the Scriptures state that the Father judges no one, they mean that He does not act directly as a judge, but rather, has entrusted all judgment to the Son. When the Scriptures state that all judgment has been committed to Jesus, they mean that Jesus has been entrusted as the Father's agent to judge. Therefore, it can be said that *both* the Father and Jesus judge—Jesus directly, as the Father's agent, and the Father indirectly, as Jesus' principal. It can also be said that neither the Father nor Jesus judge—the Father judges no one because all judgment has been committed to Jesus, and Jesus judges no one because it is not his judgment that He pronounces, but rather, it is the judgment of the word, which is the Father's. What is important is not whether we state that Jesus or the Father judges or does not judge, but rather, that we understand the symbiotic relationship between the two in the accomplishment of the Father's will.

The idea of agency, and the imputation of an agent's acts or omissions to his principal, can be found throughout scripture. For example:

> Mat 10:40 "He who receives you receives Me, and he who receives Me receives Him who sent Me.
> Luke 10:16 He who hears you hears Me, he who rejects you rejects Me, and he who rejects Me rejects Him who sent Me."
> John 12:44 Then Jesus cried out and said, "He who believes in Me, believes not in Me but in Him who sent Me. John 12:45 And he who sees Me sees Him who sent Me.
> John 13:20 Most assuredly, I say to you, he who receives whomever I send receives Me; and he who receives Me receives Him who sent Me."
> John 14:9 Jesus said to him, "Have I been with you so long, and yet you have not known Me, Philip? He who has seen Me has seen the Father; so how can you say, 'Show us the Father'? John 14:10 Do you not believe that I am in the Father, and the Father in Me? The words that I speak to you I do not speak on My own authority; but the Father who dwells in Me does the works.

CHAPTER 28. JESUS IS CRUCIFIED ON 15 NISAN IN THE SYNOPTIC GOSPELS, BUT ON 14 NISAN IN JOHN'S GOSPEL

I. CLAIM

Dr. Bilal Philips writes that in the Synoptic Gospels, "Jesus is crucified on 15 Nisan," but in the Gospel of John, "Jesus is crucified on 14 Nisan, the day of the Jewish Passover sacrifice" (p. 53).

It appears that:

- in the Synoptic Gospels, the Last Supper is held on Passover, just after sunset on 14 Nisan and into the evening of 15 Nisan. He is then crucified the next day, 15 Nisan, which is the first day of the Feast of Unleavened Bread.
- in John, Jesus is crucified on the Preparation day of Passover, which would have been held on Saturday. Therefore, the Friday of Jesus's crucifixion would have been 14 Nisan, with Passover falling the next day (Saturday).

II. INTRODUCTION TO PASSOVER AND THE FEAST OF UNLEAVENED BREAD

Passover is on 14 Nisan. It is celebrated with a Passover seder beginning on the evening after 14 Nisan, which is the evening of 15 Nisan just after sunset on 14 Nisan. The Passover seder is a Jewish ritual feast that marks the beginning of Passover.

The Feast of Unleavened Bread extends over seven days. The first and last days are high Sabbaths in which no work is undertaken. The instruction to observe the Feast of Unleavened

Bread was given in relation to Passover, which the Feast is a continuation of (Lev 23:4-8):

> Lev 23:4 These are the feasts of the Lord, holy convocations which you shall proclaim at their appointed times.
> Lev 23:5 *On the fourteenth day of the first month at twilight is the Lord's Passover.*
> Lev 23:6 *And on the fifteenth day of the same month is the Feast of Unleavened Bread to the Lord; seven days you must eat unleavened bread.*
> Lev 23:7 On the first day you shall have a holy convocation; you shall do no customary work on it.
> Lev 23:8 But you shall offer an offering made by fire to the Lord for seven days. The seventh day shall be a holy convocation; you shall do no customary work on it.

According to Chabad.org, following twilight on 14 Nisan, when the Passover was eaten, was technically the beginning of a new day, which was 15 Nisan. However, in the Jewish calendar, that evening of 15 Nisan was considered to be an *extension* of 14 Nisan[24]:

> Also note that, in a certain sense, the celebration of the 15th is considered to be an extension of the 14th. How so? With regard to sacrifices, the verse states, "And the flesh of his thanksgiving peace offering shall be eaten on the day it is offered up; he shall not leave any of it over until morning." In other words, if you were given one day to eat an offering, the day consisted of the daytime followed by its night (unlike all other purposes, for which Jewish calendar days consist of the night followed by the day). Thus, as far as sacrifices are concerned, the night after a sacrifice is brought is an extension of the day it is brought.
> Therefore, when it comes to the celebration of the Passover sacrifice, while it was eaten on the 15th, it was considered to be the same day as the 14th.

---

[24] "Why Is Passover on Nissan 15, Not Nissan 14?" available at <https://www.chabad.org/holidays/passover/pesach_cdo/aid/3283921/jewish/Why-Is-Passover-on-Nissan-15-Not-Nissan-14.htm>.

We can thus conclude that Passover was eaten following twilight on 14 Nisan and at the beginning of 15 Nisan, with the Feast of Unleavened Bread then following for 7 days.

III. SCRIPTURAL OVERVIEW

1. Chronological Overview of the Gospel Accounts

- The Last Supper (Thursday)
  o Matthew 26:17-29
  o Mark 14:12-25
  o Luke 22:7-20
  o John 13:1-38

- Gethsemane (Thursday)
  o Matthew 26:36-46
  o Mark 14:32-42
  o Luke 22:40-46

- Jesus' Arrest and Trial (Thursday night and Friday)
  o Matthew 26:47-27:26
  o Mark 14:43-15:15
  o Luke 22:47-23:25
  o John 18:2-19:16

- Jesus' Crucifixion and Death (Friday)
  o Matthew 27:27-26
  o Mark 15:16-41
  o Luke 23:26-49
  o John 19:17-30

2. Matthew's Account

a. Verses that State that Jesus Was Crucified on the First Day of the Feast of Unleavened Bread

The following verses suggest that Jesus was crucified on 15 Nisan, the first day of the Feast of Unleavened Bread:

Jesus said to His disciples that the Passover was after two days and He would be crucified (Mat 26:1-2).

On the <u>first day of the Feast of Unleavened Bread,</u>[25] <u>the
disciples came to Jesus, asking where He wanted them to
prepare to eat the Passover</u> (Mat 26:17). He said to go
into the city to a certain man and say to him that Jesus would
keep the <u>Passover</u> at his house with his disciples (Mat 26:18).
The disciples did as Jesus had directed and they
prepared the <u>Passover</u> (Mat 26:19).
<u>When it was evening,</u> He sat down with the twelve disciples
(Mat 26:20). He said that the disciple who dipped his hand
with Him in the dish would betray Him (Mat 26:21-3). Judas
asked, Is it I? Jesus replied that it was (Mat 26:25). Jesus
broke bread and gave it and the cup to the disciples (Mat
26:26-29).
They then went out to the Mount of Olives (Mat 26:30)
and Jesus came with them to Gethsemane and said to the
disciples to sit while He goes and prays (Mat 26:36). Then
Judas appeared with a great multitude with swords and clubs
(Mat 26:47). Then they took Jesus (Mat 26:50) away to
Caiaphas, the high priest (Mat 26:57), where he was charged.

Jesus is arrested and then crucified the following day, which
was a continuation of 15 Nisan in the Jewish calendar.

b. Verses that State that Jesus was Crucified on the Day of
    Preparation

Matthew states that the day of the crucifixion was the
Preparation Day and that the day after the Preparation Day the
chief priests and Pharisees asked Pilate to secure the tomb:

On the next day, <u>which followed the Day of Preparation,</u>
the chief priests and Pharisees gathered together and
said to Pilate, We remember, while Jesus was alive, He
said He will rise after three days; therefore, command that
the tomb be secured until the third day, lest His disciples steal
His body (Mat 27:62-64).

---

[25] Matthew seems to be speaking of Passover, but he refers to it as the "Feast
of Unleavened Bread."

This implies that Jesus was crucified on the Preparation Day.

3. Mark's Account

a. Verses that State that Jesus Was Crucified on the First Day of the Feast of Unleavened Bread

The following verses indicate that Jesus was crucified on the first day of the Feast of Unleavened Bread:

> On the first day of Unleavened Bread [Passover], when they killed the Passover lamb, Jesus' disciples asked Him where He wanted them to go and prepare to eat the Passover (Mark 14:12). Jesus sent two of His disciples into the city (Mark 14:13) and to request from the owner of a house the guest room for Jesus to eat the Passover with His disciples (Mark 14:14). He would show them a large upper room to make ready for them (Mark 14:15). The disciples went to the city and prepared the Passover (Mark 14:16).
> They sung a hymn and went to the Mount of Olives (Mark 14:26), where Jesus predicted that before the rooster crows twice, Peter would deny Him three times (Mark 14:30). Then they came to Gethsemane, where Jesus told His disciples to sit while he prays (Mark 14:32).
> While Jesus was speaking, Judas and the chief priests, scribes and elders came with a great multitude with swords and clubs and arrested Jesus (Mark 14:43-51). He was brought before the Sanhedrin, where He admitted to being the Son of God (Mark 14:53-64).

Jesus is then crucified the following day, which was a continuation of 15 Nisan on the Jewish calendar.

b. Verses that State that Jesus was Crucified on the Day of Preparation

Mark states that the evening of the crucifixion was the Preparation Day before the Sabbath (Mark 15:42):

> When evening had come, because it was the Preparation Day, that is, the day before the Sabbath (Mark 15:42), Joseph of Arimathea, a prominent council member, who was waiting for the kingdom of God, went in to Pilate and asked for the

body of Jesus (Mark 15:43). Pilate granted the body to Joseph (Mark 15:45). Joseph bought fine linen, took Him down, wrapped Him in the linen, laid Him in a tomb and rolled a stone against the door of the tomb (Mark 15:46). Mary Magdalene and Mary the mother of Joses observed where He was laid (Mark 15:47).

This implies that Jesus was crucified on either the Preparation Day (Friday) or the Preparation Day to Passover. However, the Bible does not make a reference to a "Preparation Day" for Passover, and so this latter option is unlikely.

4. Luke's Account

a. Verses that State that Jesus was Crucified on the First Day of the Feast of Unleavened Bread

The following verses indicate that the Last Supper was the Passover seder and Jesus was crucified on the first day of the Feast of Unleavened Bread:

> As the Feast of Unleavened Bread, which is called Passover, drew near (Luke 22:1), the chief priests and scribes sought to kill Jesus (Luke 22:2). Satan entered Judas Iscariot (Luke 22:3), who went to the chief priests and officers of the temple guard to betray Jesus in the absence of the crowds (Luke 22:4-6).
> The Day of Unleavened Bread [Passover], when the Passover lamb had to be sacrificed, then came (Luke 22:7). He sent Peter and John to go and prepare the Passover so that they may eat (Luke 22:8). He told them that when they entered the city, they would meet a man carrying a pitcher of water and to follow him into the house that he enters (Luke 22:10) and to prepare the Passover in the guest room (Luke 22:11-13).
> Jesus sat down with the twelve Apostles (Luke 22:14) and said that He fervently desired to eat the Passover with them before He suffered (Luke 22:15) and that He will no longer eat of it until it is fulfilled in the kingdom of God (Luke 22:16). He gave them the cup (Luke 22:17) and said He would not drink of the fruit of the vine again until the kingdom of God comes (Luke 22:18). He broke the bread and gave it to them, saying, This is My body given for you; do

188 Bible Contradictions and Their Resolutions

this in remembrance of Me (Luke 22:19). He also took the cup and said, This is the new covenant in My blood, which is poured out for you (Luke 22:20).

Jesus and His disciples went to the Mount of Olives (Luke 22:39). Then Judas appeared with a multitude and had Jesus arrested (Luke 22:47-53). They took Jesus to the home of the high priest.

According to Luke, the last supper was the Passover Seder, and Jesus represented the Passover sacrificial lamb, whose body and blood was given for His followers. Jesus, following His arrest, was crucified the following day, which was a continuation of 15 Nisan in the Jewish calendar.

b. Verses that State that Jesus was Crucified on the Day of Preparation

According to Luke, Joseph took Jesus's body down and buried it on the Preparation Day of the Sabbath:

Jesus was crucified (Luke 23:26) and died on the cross (Luke 24:44-49). A man named Joseph asked for Jesus' body (Luke 23:50-52). He took the body down, wrapped it in linen and laid it in a tomb (Luke 23:53). That day was the Preparation and the Sabbath drew near (Luke 23:54).

This implies that Jesus was crucified on the Preparation Day, which would have been a Friday.

5. John's Account

According to John, Jesus was crucified on the Preparation Day:

- John states, "Now before the Feast of the Passover, when Jesus knew that His hour had come that He should depart from this world to the Father, having loved His own who were in the world, He loved them to the end. And supper being ended, the devil having already put it into the heart of Judas Iscariot, Simon's son, to betray Him" (John 13:1-2). It is unclear whether this meal was the Passover meal or a meal "before the Feast of the Passover" (John 13:1).

- Jesus was arrested on Thursday evening and the Jews led Jesus from Caiaphas to the palace of the Roman governor in the early morning [on Friday], but the Jews did not enter the palace to avoid ceremonial uncleanliness and to be able to eat the Passover (John 18:28), which would have presumably been on Saturday, with the Passover seder eaten on Friday evening.
- Pilate came out to the Jews and questioned them and then questioned Jesus, ultimately concluding that he found no fault with Jesus (John 18:29-38), yet the Jews cried out against Jesus (John 19:12). Pilate brought Jesus out and sat down in the judgment seat (John 19:13). "[I]t was the Preparation Day of the Passover, and about the sixth hour" (John 19:14).[26]
- Pilate delivered Jesus to be crucified and the soldiers took hold of Him (John 19:16). The soldiers crucified Jesus (John 19:23) on Friday, the Preparation Day.
- "[B]ecause it was the Preparation Day, that the bodies should not remain on the cross on the Sabbath (for that Sabbath was a high day), the Jews asked Pilate that their legs might be broken, and that they might be taken away" (John 19:31).

John states the following:

It was just before the Passover feast (John 13:1). The evening meal was being served (John 13:2) and Jesus washed the feet of His Apostles (John 13:4-11).

Jesus went out with His disciples over the Brook Kidron, where there was a garden (John 18:1). Judas, having received a detachment of troops and officers from the chief priests and Pharisees, came there with torches and weapons (John 18:3). Jesus was arrested (John 18:12). They led Him away to

---

[26] The sixth hour could mean noon or midnight, but if John used the supposed Roman time, it would mean 6:00 am or 6:00 pm.

Annas, the father-in-law of Caiaphas, the high priest that year (John 18:13).

Then the Jews led Jesus from Caiaphas to the palace of the Roman governor and it was early morning [Friday], but the Jews did not enter the palace to avoid ceremonial uncleanliness and to be able to eat the Passover (John 18:28). Pilate came out to the Jews and questioned them and then questioned Jesus, ultimately concluding that he found no fault with Jesus (John 18:29-38). He offered to release Jesus or Barabbas, but they chose for Barabbas to be released (John 18:39-40).

The Jews cried out, saying that if Pilate released Jesus, he was against Caesar, for Jesus made Himself a King (John 19:12). When Pilate heard this, he brought Jesus out and sat down in the judgment seat (John 19:13). It was the Preparation Day of the Passover at about the sixth hour (John 19:14).

Pilate delivered Jesus to be crucified and the soldiers took hold of Him (John 19:16). The soldiers crucified Jesus (John 19:23). Jesus declared, It is finished, and gave up His spirit (John 19:30).

Because it was the Preparation Day, so that the bodies not remain on the cross on the Sabbath (for that Sabbath was a high day), the Jews asked Pilate to have the legs broken and the bodies taken down (John 19:31).

IV. EXPLANATION: "PASSOVER" IS USED INTERCHANGEABLY WITH "FEAST OF UNLEAVENED BREAD"

1. GotQuestions.org Explanation

According to GotQuestions.org,[27]

One objection to the above chronology is based on John 18:28, which says, "The Jewish leaders took Jesus from Caiaphas to the palace of the Roman governor. By now it was early morning, and to avoid ceremonial uncleanness they did

---

[27] "If Jesus was crucified on the Day of Preparation, why had He already eaten the Passover meal?" available at <https://www.gotquestions.org/Day-of-Preparation.html>.

not enter the palace, because they wanted to be able to eat the Passover." At first glance, it seems that, whereas Jesus had eaten the Passover the night before, the Jewish leaders had not yet eaten the Passover—they still "wanted to be able to eat" it after Jesus was arrested. To reconcile this verse with the Synoptic narratives, we must remember this: Passover was the first day of the week-long Feast of Unleavened Bread.

The Feast (or Festival) of Unleavened Bread (Chag HaMatzot) lasted for a full week, from Nissan 15 to Nissan 22. The first day of Unleavened Bread coincided with the day of Passover. Because of the close relation between Passover and the Feast of Unleavened Bread, the whole week was sometimes referred to as "Passover." The two holidays were (and still are) considered a single celebration. This explains John 18:28. *The Jewish leaders had already eaten the Passover proper, but there still remained other sacrifices to be made and meals to be eaten.* They were unwilling to defile themselves (Pilate's palace contained leaven) because it would disqualify them from participating in the remainder of the week's ceremonies (see Leviticus 23:8).

The book of Chronicles confirms that there were other meals eaten throughout the week of the Feast of Unleavened Bread:

2Ch 30:13 Now many people, a very great assembly, gathered at Jerusalem to keep the Feast of Unleavened Bread in the second month.

2Ch 30:14 They arose and took away the altars that were in Jerusalem, and they took away all the incense altars and cast them into the Brook Kidron.

2Ch 30:15 Then they slaughtered the Passover lambs on the fourteenth day of the second month. The priests and the Levites were ashamed, and sanctified themselves, and brought the burnt offerings to the house of the Lord.

2Ch 30:16 They stood in their place according to their custom, according to the Law of Moses the man of God; the priests sprinkled the blood received from the hand of the Levites.

2Ch 30:17 For there were many in the assembly who had not sanctified themselves; therefore the Levites had charge of the slaughter of the Passover lambs for everyone who was not clean, to sanctify them to the Lord.

2Ch 30:18 For a multitude of the people, many from Ephraim, Manasseh, Issachar, and Zebulun, had not cleansed themselves, yet they ate the Passover contrary to what was written. But Hezekiah prayed for them, saying, "May the good Lord provide atonement for everyone

2Ch 30:19 who prepares his heart to seek God, the Lord God of his fathers, though he is not cleansed according to the purification of the sanctuary."

2Ch 30:20 And the Lord listened to Hezekiah and healed the people.

2Ch 30:21 So the children of Israel who were present at Jerusalem kept the Feast of Unleavened Bread seven days with great gladness; and the Levites and the priests praised the Lord day by day, singing to the Lord, accompanied by loud instruments.

2Ch 30:22 And Hezekiah gave encouragement to all the Levites who taught the good knowledge of the Lord; and they ate throughout the feast seven days, offering peace offerings and making confession to the Lord God of their fathers.

2. Brant Pitre's Explanation

Moreover, Footnote 68 on page 214 of Brant Pitre's *Jesus and the Jewish Roots of the Eucharist* states:

I should note here that many modern scholars doubt that the Last Supper was in fact a Jewish Passover meal, despite the explicit testimony of Matthew, Mark, and Luke. This doubt is primarily rooted in an apparent chronological contradiction between John's Gospel and the Synoptics. For an overview of the problem, see Jeremias, *The Eucharistic Words of Jews*, 15-88. In a longer study on Jesus and the Last Supper still in preparation (Grand Rapids: Eerdmans, forthcoming), I will argue that the apparent contradiction is based on a misinterpretation of the word Passover in John's Gospel, and that all four Gospels do in fact identify the Last Supper as a Passover meal. For this solution, see e.g., Craig L. Blomberg, The Historical Reliability of John's Gospel: Issues & Commentary) (Downers Grove, Ill.: InterVarsity, 2001), 193-94, 238-39, 246-47; Barry D. Smith, "The Chronology of the Last Supper," Westminster Theological Journal 53 (1991): 29-45; C. C. Torrey, "The Date of the Crucifixion According to the Fourth Gospel," Journal of Biblical Literature 50 (1931): 227-41; idem, "In the Fourth Gospel the Last Supper Was a Passover Meal," Jewish Quarterly Review 42 (1951-52): 237-50; Cornelius a Lapide, SJ., Commentary on the Four Gospels, 4 volumes (Fitzwilliam, N.H.: Loreto, 2008 [orig. ca. 1637]), 2:522-26; 4:512- 513; Thomas Aquinas, Summa Theologica, Part III, Q. 46, An. 9.

Brant Pitre's footnote focuses on the fact that John did not mean to circumscribe his use of the term "Passover" in his Gospel to the Thursday of 14 Nisan. Rather, he uses it more broadly:

- John states that the Jews did not enter the palace to avoid ceremonial uncleanliness and to be able to eat the <u>Passover</u> (John 18:28). Here, John is conflating Passover with the Feast of Unleavened Bread. On the evening of 15 Nisan, the Friday after Passover, the Jews would have had another meal, and it was this meal to which John was referring, though that day was not technically Passover as narrowly defined in Leviticus 23:5.
- John states that it was the <u>Preparation Day of the Passover</u> at about the sixth hour (John 19:14). Again, John is not referring to 14 Nisan, but rather, to the preparation day of the week of Passover, which would have bene the preparation day of the weekly Sabbath. This is because by the time of Jesus' coming, Passover and the Feast of Unleavened Bread were conflated, and referring to one referring to another. John could have just has easily written, "It was the Preparation Day of the Sabbath of the Feast of Unleavened Bread."
- John states that because it was the <u>Preparation Day</u>, so that the bodies not remain on the cross on the Sabbath (for that Sabbath was a high day), the Jews asked Pilate to have the legs broken and the bodies taken down (John 19:31). However, John does not specify that it was the Preparation Day of Passover. Here, Preparation Day would have been referring to the preparation day of the weekly Sabbath (*i.e.*, the Friday before the Sabbath).

3. The Conflation of Passover and the Feast of Unleavened Bread as per Melanie J. Wright

In *Studying Judaism: The Critical Issues*, Melanie J. Wright writes:

> At the same time, since the destruction of the Jerusalem temple meant that sacrifices were no longer possible, they shifted emphasis from the lamp to the unleavened bread (matzah) as the primary symbol of the holiday.

This implies that the shift would have occurred after the destruction of the first Jewish template (Solomon's temple) in 586 BC, or possibly following the disrepair of the second temple (Zerubbabel's temple) in 20 BC or the destruction of the third temple (Herod's temple) in 70 AD, which was destroyed in 586 BC by the Babylonians under Nebuchadnezzar, when they burned Jerusalem.

4. Current Usage

One Chabad[28] Jew that this author consulted confirmed that when modern Jews in America refer to Passover, they are not referring to 14 Nisan only. Rather, they are referring to the entire 8-week holiday consisting of both Passover and the Feast of Unleavened Bread. He wrote, "Passover refers to all 8 days." He further stated that modern Jews no longer use the term "Feast of Unleavened Bread." Professor Michael Satlow reiterates this idea in his post, "Passover and the Festival of Matzot: Synthesizing Two Holidays."[29] He writes:

> The holiday that today we call Passover had its origins as two separate holidays, Passover proper and the Festival of Unleavened Bread, chag ha-matzot.

Professor Satlow therefore confirms that today, what is called Passover actually combined both Passover and the Feast of

---

[28] Chabad is an Orthodox Jewish Hasidic movement.
[29] "Passover and the Festival of Matzot: Synthesizing Two Holidays," TheTorah.com, available at <https://www.thetorah.com/article/passover-and-the-festival-of-matzot-synthesizing-two-holidays>.

Unleavened Bread. As discussed below, it appears that this was the case as early as the days of Jesus, if not earlier.

5. Further Scriptural Support

So far, we have attempted to explain the apparent contradiction by arguing that the reference to the Jews' eating the Passover in John 18:28 should not be read narrowly as referring to the Passover meal following sunset on 14 Nisan, but rather, to both Passover and the Feast of Unleavened Bread more broadly. The Synoptic Evangelists used the term "Passover" to refer to both Passover and the Feast of Unleavened Bread, which, by the time of Jesus, had become interchangeable terms. The Evangelists used the terms "Passover" and "Feast of Unleavened Bread" interchangeably:

- Matthew states that on the first day of the "Feast of Unleavened Bread," the disciples came to Jesus, asking where He wanted them to prepare to eat the Passover (Mat 26:17). However, it could not have been the first day of the Feast of Unleavened Bread when the disciples came to Jesus because the Jews prepare the Passover on Passover, which is 14 Nisan, not on the Feast of Unleavened Bread, which is 15 Nisan. Therefore, by "Feast of Unleavened Bread," John must have been referring to Passover.
- Mark states that on the first day of "Unleavened Bread," when they killed the Passover lamb, Jesus' disciples asked Him where He wanted them to go and prepare to eat the Passover (Mark 14:12). Again, it could not have been the first Day of the Feast of Unleavened Bread (15 Nisan) when the Passover was prepared; the Passover is prepared on Passover (14 Nisan) to be eaten after twilight on 14 Nisan. Mark is therefore conflating Passover with the Feast of Unleavened Bread.
- Luke states that "the Feast of Unleavened Bread drew near, which is called Passover" (Luke 22:1). He further states "then came the Day of Unleavened Bread, when the Passover must be killed" (Luke 22:7). Again, the

Passover lamb is killed on Passover, not on the Feast of Unleavened Bread, which follows Passover. Luke is conflating the two holidays.

Moreover, other books throughout the Old and New Testaments refer to Passover and the Feast of Unleavened Bread interchangeably:

- Ezekiel states, "In the first month, on the fourteenth day of the month, you shall observe the *Passover*, a feast of *seven days; unleavened bread shall be eaten*" (Eze 45:21).
- Acts 12:3-4 states, "And because he saw that it pleased the Jews, he proceeded further to seize Peter also. Now it was during the *Days of Unleavened Bread*. So when he had arrested him, he put him in prison, and delivered him to four squads of soldiers to keep him, intending to bring him before the people after *Passover*."

6. How to Properly Read References to "Passover" in John

On the basis of the foregoing, we should not read the references to "Passover" in John as strictly referring to Passover proper; rather, we should read these as references to Passover and the Feast of Unleavened Bread as a continuous, eight-day holiday that began on 14 Nisan and concluded on 21 Nisan. In this light, we can read the following verses from John in the following ways:

a.   The Jews Eating the Passover

Jesus was arrested on Thursday evening and the Jews led Jesus from Caiaphas to the palace of the Roman governor in the early morning [on Friday], but the Jews did not enter the palace to avoid ceremonial uncleanliness and to <u>be able to eat the Passover</u> (John 18:28).

Here, John is not referring to the Passover meal that would have been eaten after twilight on 14 Nisan (Thursday evening), but rather, to one of the meals of the Feast of Unleavened Bread, which would have been celebrated throughout the week of 15-21 Nisan. Leviticus states that for seven days during the Feast of Unleavened Bread, unleavened bread must be eaten

(Lev 23:6). Numbers states that during the Feast of Unleavened Bread, unleavened bread shall be eaten for seven days (Num 28:17). Both books refer to the Jews eating unleavened bread throughout the week, so there were meals that would have been eaten during the week in accordance with the scriptural mandate to eat unleavened bread.

Numbers 28:16-25 describes the sacrifices to be offered on each day of the Feast of Unleavened Bread as follows:

- On the first day you shall present an offering made by fire as a burnt offering to the Lord: two young bulls, one ram, and seven lambs in their first year and without blemish (Num 28:19).
- With each bull offer a grain offering of three-tenths of an ephah of flour mixed with oil; with the ram, two-tenths (Num 28:20) and with each of the seven lambs, one-tenth (Num 28:21)
- One goat as a sin offering (Num 28:22).
- You shall offer the food of the offering made by fire daily for seven days, as a sweet aroma to the Lord; it shall be offered besides the regular burnt offering and its drink offering (Num 28:24).

Some of these offerings were eaten by both the priests and the Jews. Offerings were often cooked and most of it eaten by the offerer, with parts given to the Kohen priests and small parts burned on the altar of the Temple in Jerusalem. In certain special cases, all of the offering was given only to God, such as in the case of the scapegoat.[30] Multiple verses from the Old Testament indicate that the Jews ate the sacrifices:

Lev 7:19 'The flesh that touches any unclean thing shall not be eaten. It shall be burned with fire. *And as for the clean flesh, all who are clean may eat of it*.

---

[30] Tracey R. Rich, "Qorbanot: Sacrifices and Offerings," *Judaism 101* (1998–2011); Morris Jastrow, et al. "Azazel" Jewish Encyclopedia (1906).

Lev 7:20 But *the person who eats the flesh of the sacrifice of the peace offering that belongs to the Lord, while he is unclean, that person shall be cut off from his people*.

Exo 12:6 Now you shall keep it until the fourteenth day of the same month. Then the whole assembly of the congregation of Israel shall kill it at twilight.
Exo 12:7 And they shall take some of the blood and put it on the two doorposts and on the lintel of the houses where they eat it.
Exo 12:8 Then *they shall eat the flesh on that night; roasted in fire, with unleavened bread and with bitter herbs they shall eat it*.
Exo 12:9 *Do not eat it raw*, nor boiled at all with water, but roasted in fire--its head with its legs and its entrails.
Exo 12:10 *You shall let none of it remain until morning*, and what remains of it until morning you shall burn with fire.

Num 9:9 Then the Lord spoke to Moses, saying,
Num 9:10 "Speak to the children of Israel, saying: 'If anyone of you or your posterity is unclean because of a corpse, or is far away on a journey, he may still keep the Lord's Passover.
Num 9:11 On the fourteenth day of the second month, at twilight, they may keep it. *They shall eat it with unleavened bread and bitter herbs*.
Num 9:12 *They shall leave none of it until morning*, nor break one of its bones. According to all the ordinances of the Passover they shall keep it.

As per these verses, the Jews ate of the sacrifices that they brought to the Lord. Therefore, during the Feast of Unleavened Bread, they would have also partaken in these meals, in addition to eating the unleavened bread that they were commanded to eat. Because the terms "Passover" and "Feast of Unleavened Bread" were used interchangeably at the time of Jesus, John's reference to eating "the Passover" in John 18:28 should be read as eating one of the meals during the week of the Feast of Unleavened Bread.

b. Trial of Jesus on the Preparation Day of the Passover

John wrote that Pilate came out to the Jews and questioned them and then questioned Jesus, ultimately concluding that he found no fault with Jesus (John 18:29-38), yet the Jews cried out against Jesus (John 19:12). Pilate brought Jesus out and sat down in the judgment seat (John 19:13). He writes, "it was the Preparation Day of the Passover, and about the sixth hour" (John 19:14).[31]

Here, "Preparation Day" refers to the Friday before the Sabbath. On the Preparation Day, Jews prepared for the Sabbath, since they were unable to do any work on the Sabbath. The Preparation Day cannot mean the day prior to Passover (i.e., 13 Nisan) because "Preparation Day" has no such use in the Old or New Testaments. It can therefore only refer to the Preparation Day of the Sabbath. By "Preparation Day of the Passover," John means the Preparation Day of the Sabbath of Passover week (i.e., the Preparation Day of the Sabbath that fell during the week of Passover and the Feast of Unleavened Bread).

c.   Breaking the Legs on the Preparation Day

John wrote that "because it was the Preparation Day, that the bodies should not remain on the cross on the Sabbath (for that Sabbath was a high day), the Jews asked Pilate that their legs might be broken, and that they might be taken away" (John 19:31).

This verse makes clear that the "Preparation Day" referenced in John 19:14 is the Preparation Day of the Sabbath (i.e., Good Friday), not a preparation day for Passover.

The verse further makes clear that the Friday of Jesus's crucifixion was *both* the Preparation Day of the weekly Sabbath as well as a high Sabbath—it was the first day of the Feast of Unleavened Bread, or 15 Nisan. John writes that the "Sabbath was a high day").

---

[31] The sixth hour could mean noon or midnight, but if John used the supposed Roman time, it would mean 6:00 am or 6:00 pm.

CHAPTER 29. LEVITICUS STATES THAT PASSOVER AND THE FEAST OF UNLEAVENED BREAD ARE SEPARATE HOLIDAYS, BUT THE GOSPELS CONFLATE THEM

I. OVERVIEW

Leviticus clearly distinguishes between Passover, which is on 14 Nisan, and the Feast of Unleavened Bread, which starts on 15 Nisan and goes through 22 Nisan:

> Lev 23:5 On the fourteenth day of the first month at twilight is the Lord's Passover.
> Lev 23:6 And on the fifteenth day of the same month is the Feast of Unleavened Bread to the Lord; seven days you must eat unleavened bread.

However, the Gospel writers conflate Passover with the Feast of Unleavened Bread, treating Passover as the first day of the Feast of Unleavened Bread rather than as the day preceding the first day of the Feast of Unleavened Bread. For example:

- The Gospel of Matthew states that "on the first day of the Feast of Unleavened Bread the disciples came to Jesus, saying to Him, 'Where do You want us to prepare for You to eat the Passover?'" (Mat 26:17). The first day of the Feast of Unleavened Bread was 15 Nisan. Matthew goes on to state, "When evening had come, He sat down with the twelve" (Mat 26:20). Therefore, during the day of 15 Nisan (i.e., before sunset), the disciples asked Jesus where He wanted to prepare the Passover. Then evening came, and it would have been 16 Nisan. Yet if they were eating the Passover seder, it should have been just after twilight on 14 Nisan, which would have been 15 Nisan.

- The Gospel of Mark states that on the first day of Unleavened Bread, when they killed the Passover lamb, Jesus' disciples asked Him where He wanted them to go and prepare to eat the Passover (Mark 14:12). This would have been during the day on 15 Nisan, since Mark goes on to state that "In the evening He came with the twelve [and] they sat and ate" (Mark 14:17-18). It thus appears in this account that Passover was eaten after twilight on 15 Nisan, at the start of 16 Nisan, rather than after twilight on 14 Nisan, at the start of 15 Nisan.

- Luke writes that as the Feast of Unleavened Bread, which is called Passover, drew near (Luke 22:1), the chief priests and scribes sought to kill Jesus (Luke 22:2). It also equates Passover with the Feast of Unleavened Bread, even though Leviticus clearly distinguishes between them. Luke also writes that the Passover lamb had to be sacrificed on the Day of Unleavened Bread (Luke 22:7). In reality, however, the Passover lamb had to be sacrificed on Passover (14 Nisan) so that it could be eaten after twilight on 14 Nisan, at the start of 15 Nisan, which is the first day of the Feast of Unleavened Bread. If the Passover lamb were sacrificed on the Day of Unleavened Bread, then there would be no sacrificial lamb on 14 Nisan to be eaten at the Passover seder.

II. PROPOSED EXPLANATION 1: LEVITICUS 23 IS DESCRIPTIVE RATHER THAN PRESCRIPTIVE

1. Overview

Passover, or Pesach, was a holiday that was originally celebrated locally. It became a pilgrimage festival around the time of Solomon's Temple. At about that time, the two holidays became intertwined or conflated.

The best way to explain this is that traditions can change over time. Events like the exile, destruction of the first temple, construction of the second temple, and operation of local shrines (Dan and Bethel) all influence the ways in which festivals are observed. Some texts, though they appear prescriptive, may actually be describing the way things are.

When conditions shift, worship practices may also adjust to meet the needs of the new situation.

2. Response

While it may be the case that some texts are descriptive rather than prescriptive, in the case of the celebration of Passover on 14 Nisan and the Feast of Unleavened Bread on 15 Nisan, the Scriptures appear prescriptive, not descriptive (i.e, "you shall proclaim at their appointed times"):

> Lev 23:4 'These are the feasts of the Lord, holy convocations which you shall proclaim at their appointed times.
> Lev 23:5 On the fourteenth day of the first month at twilight is the Lord's Passover.
> Lev 23:6 And on the fifteenth day of the same month is the Feast of Unleavened Bread to the Lord; seven days you must eat unleavened bread.
> Lev 23:7 On the first day you shall have a holy convocation; you shall do no customary work on it.
> Lev 23:8 But you shall offer an offering made by fire to the Lord for seven days. The seventh day shall be a holy convocation; you shall do no customary work on it.' "

Therefore, if the Jews (including Jesus) were not celebrating the feasts as God commanded, with Passover celebrated after twilight on 14 Nisan and the Feast of Unleavened Bread celebrated for seven days beginning on 15 Nisan, then either the Jews did not comply with how God commanded the Scriptures to be celebrated or God changed His law as to how to celebrate the feasts. If the latter is the case, it would indicate that God's law is not timeless and unchanging.

III. PROPOSED EXPLANATION 2

A second proposed explanation is that the Jews observed the dates, but they referred to them differently. In other words, Passover was the holiday that was celebrated on 14 Nisan and the Feast of Unleavened Bread began on 15 Nisan. The Jews celebrated both holidays, but they simply did not observe the distinction with respect to referring to the two holidays as dictated in Leviticus because, over time, usage had changed.

This explanation likely aligns with the explanation given above under "Potential Explanation: 'Passover' Is Used Interchangeably with 'Feast of Unleavened Bread'" and, more specifically, the explanation referring to the destruction of the Jerusalem temple under "The Conflation of Passover and the Feast of Unleavened Bread as per Melanie J. Wright."

CHAPTER 30. ACCOUNTS OF THE RESURRECTION (MAT 28, MARK 16, LUKE 24, JOHN 20)

I. TEXTS OF THE FOUR GOSPEL ACCOUNTS

Matthew	Mark	Luke	John
Mat 28:1 Now after the Sabbath, as the first day of the week began to dawn, Mary Magdalene and the other Mary came to see the tomb. Mat 28:2 And behold, there was a great earthquake; for an angel of the Lord descended from heaven, and came and rolled back the stone from the	Mark 16:1 Now when the Sabbath was past, Mary Magdalene, Mary the mother of James, and Salome bought spices, that they might come and anoint Him. Mark 16:2 Very early in the morning, on the first day of the week, they came to the tomb when the sun	Luke 24:1 Now on the first day of the week, very early in the morning, they, and certain other women with them, came to the tomb bringing the spices which they had prepared. Luke 24:2 But they found the stone rolled away from the tomb. Luke 24:3 Then they went in and	John 20:1 Now the first day of the week Mary Magdalene went to the tomb early, while it was still dark, and saw that the stone had been taken away from the tomb. John 20:2 Then she ran and came to Simon Peter, and to the other disciple, whom Jesus loved, and said to them, "They have

door, and sat on it.

Mat 28:3 His countenance was like lightning, and his clothing as white as snow.

Mat 28:4 And the guards shook for fear of him, and became like dead men.

Mat 28:5 But the angel answered and said to the women, *"Do not be afraid, for I know that you seek Jesus who was crucified.*

Mat 28:6 He is not here; for He is risen, as He said. Come, see the place where the Lord lay.

Mat 28:7

had risen.

Mark 16:3 And they said among themselves, "Who will roll away the stone from the door of the tomb for us?"

Mark 16:4 But when they looked up, they saw that the stone had been rolled away—for it was very large.

Mark 16:5 And entering the tomb, they saw a young man clothed in a long white robe sitting on the right side; and they were alarmed.

Mark

did not find the body of the Lord Jesus.

Luke 24:4 And it happened, as they were greatly perplexed about this, that behold, two men stood by them in shining garments.

Luke 24:5 Then, as they were afraid and bowed their faces to the earth, they said to them, "Why do you seek the living among the dead?

Luke 24:6 He is not here, but is risen! Remember how He spoke to you

taken away the Lord out of the tomb, and we do not know where they have laid Him."

John 20:3 Peter therefore went out, and the other disciple, and were going to the tomb.

John 20:4 So they both ran together, and the other disciple outran Peter and came to the tomb first.

John 20:5 And he, stooping down and looking in, saw the linen cloths lying there; yet he did not go in.

John 20:6 Then Simon Peter came, following

And go quickly and tell His disciples that He is risen from the dead, and indeed He is going before you into Galilee; there you will see Him. Behold, I have told you."

Mat 28:8 So they went out quickly from the tomb with fear and great joy, and ran to bring His disciples word.

Mat 28:9 **And as they went to tell His disciples, behold, Jesus met them, saying, "Rejoice!" So they came and held Him by the**

16:6 But he said to them, "Do not be alarmed. You seek Jesus of Nazareth, who was crucified. He is risen! He is not here. See the place where they laid Him.

Mark 16:7 But go, tell His disciples—and Peter—that He is going before you into Galilee; there you will see Him, as He said to you."

Mark 16:8 So they went out quickly and fled from the tomb, for they trembled and were amazed. And they said nothing

when He was still in Galilee,

Luke 24:7 saying, 'The Son of Man must be delivered into the hands of sinful men, and be crucified, and the third day rise again.' "

Luke 24:8 And they remembered His words.

Luke 24:9 Then they returned from the tomb and told all these things to the eleven and to all the rest.

Luke 24:10 It was Mary Magdalene, Joanna, Mary the mother of James, and the other women with them, who

him, and went into the tomb; and he saw the linen cloths lying there,

John 20:7 and the handkerchief that had been around His head, not lying with the linen cloths, but folded together in a place by itself.

John 20:8 Then the other disciple, who came to the tomb first, went in also; and he saw and believed.

John 20:9 For as yet they did not know the Scripture, that He must rise again from the dead.

John 20:10 Then

feet and worshiped Him.

Mat 28:10 Then Jesus said to them, "Do not be afraid. Go and tell My brethren to go to Galilee, and there they will see Me."

to anyone, for they were afraid.

Mark 16:9 Now when He rose early on the first day of the week, He appeared first to Mary Magdalene, out of whom He had cast seven demons.

Mark 16:10 She went and told those who had been with Him, as they mourned and wept.

Mark 16:11 And when they heard that He was alive and had been seen by her, they did not believe.

Mark 16:12 After

told these things to the apostles.

Luke 24:11 And their words seemed to them like idle tales, and they did not believe them.

Luke 24:12 But Peter arose and ran to the tomb; and stooping down, he saw the linen cloths lying by themselves; and he departed, marveling to himself at what had happened.

the disciples went away again to their own homes.

John 20:11 But Mary stood outside by the tomb weeping, and as she wept she stooped down and looked into the tomb.

John 20:12 And she saw two angels in white sitting, one at the head and the other at the feet, where the body of Jesus had lain.

John 20:13 Then they said to her, "Woman, why are you weeping?" She said to them, "Because

	that, He appeared in another form to two of them as they walked and went into the country.		they have taken away my Lord, and I do not know where they have laid Him."
	Mark 16:13 And they went and told it to the rest, but they did not believe them either.		John 20:14 Now when she had said this, she turned around and saw Jesus standing there, and did not know that it was Jesus.
	Mark 16:14 Later He appeared to the eleven as they sat at the table; and He rebuked their unbelief and hardness of heart, because they did not believe those who had seen Him after He had risen.		John 20:15 Jesus said to her, "Woman, why are you weeping? Whom are you seeking?" She, supposing Him to be the gardener, said to Him, "Sir, if You have carried Him away, tell me where You have laid Him, and I
	Mark 16:15 And He said to them, "Go		

	into all the world and preach the gospel to every creature.	will take Him away."
	Mark 16:16 He who believes and is baptized will be saved; but he who does not believe will be condemned.	John 20:16 Jesus said to her, "Mary!" She turned and said to Him, "Rabboni!" (which is to say, Teacher).
	Mark 16:17 And these signs will follow those who believe: In My name they will cast out demons; they will speak with new tongues;	John 20:17 Jesus said to her, "Do not cling to Me, for I have not yet ascended to My Father; but go to My brethren and say to them, 'I am ascending to My Father and your Father, and to My God and your God.' "
	Mark 16:18 they will take up serpents; and if they drink anything deadly, it will by no	John 20:18 Mary Magdalene came and told the disciples that she had seen the Lord, and that He

	means hurt them; they will lay hands on the sick, and they will recover."		had spoken these things to her.

II. SYNCHRONIZATION OF THE FOUR ACCOUNTS

1. Original Synchronization (c. 2014)

	Matthew	Mark	Luke	John
Angel rolls away stone	Mat 28:2 And behold, there was a great earthquake; for an angel of the Lord descended from heaven, and came and rolled back the stone from the door, and sat on it. Mat 28:3 His countenanc			

	Matthew	Mark	Luke	John
	e was like lightning, and his clothing as white as snow. Mat 28:4 And the guards shook for fear of him, and became like dead men.			
Mary Magdalene went to the tomb before the other women[32]				John 20:1 Now the first day of the week Mary Magdalene went to the tomb early, while it was still dark, and

[32] This may explain the following: (i) John is the only one to mention the departure while it was still dark, thus lending credence to the idea that Mary departed before the other women; (ii) John was one of the two disciples (the other being Peter) who was informed by Mary and then ran to the tomb, which may explain why Matthew, the other direct eyewitness evangelist, did not report this.

	Matthew	Mark	Luke	John
				saw that the stone had been taken away from the tomb.
Mary the mother of James, Salome and the other women join Magdalene at the tomb.	Mat 28:1 Now after the Sabbath, as the first day of the week began to dawn, Mary Magdalene and the other Mary came to see the tomb.	Mark 16:1 Now when the Sabbath was past, Mary Magdalene, Mary the mother of James, and Salome bought spices, that they might come and anoint Him. Mark 16:2 Very early in the morning, on the first day of the	Luke 24:1 Now on the first day of the week, very early in the morning, they, and certain other women with them, came to the tomb bringing the spices which they had prepared. Luke 24:2 But they found the stone rolled away from the	

	Matthew	Mark	Luke	John
		week, they came to the tomb when the sun had risen. Mark 16:3 And they said among themselves, "Who will roll away the stone from the door of the tomb for us?" Mark 16:4 But when they looked up, they saw that the stone had been rolled away— for it was very large.	tomb. Luke 24:10 It was Mary Magdalene, Joanna, Mary the mother of James, and the other women with them, who told these things to the apostles.	

	Matthew	**Mark**	**Luke**	**John**
Mary Magdalene leaves the tomb and comes to Simon Peter and John, before the angel(s) appear to the other women				John 20:2 Then she ran and came to Simon Peter, and to the other disciple, whom Jesus loved.
One (or two) angels speak	Mat 28:5 But the angel answered and said to the women, *"Do not be afraid, for I know that you seek Jesus who was crucified. Mat 28:6 He is not here; for He is risen, as He said. Come, see*	Mark 16:5 And entering the tomb, they saw a young man clothed in a long white robe sitting on the right side; and they were alarmed. Mark 16:6 But he said to them, "*Do*	Luke 24:3 Then they went in and did not find the body of the Lord Jesus. Luke 24:4 And it happened, as they were greatly perplexed about this, that behold, two men	

	Matthew	Mark	Luke	John
	the place where the Lord lay. Mat 28:7 *And go quickly and tell His disciples that He is risen from the dead, and indeed He is going before you into Galilee; there you will see Him. Behold, I have told you."*	*not be alarmed. You seek Jesus of Nazareth, who was crucified. He is risen! He is not here. See the place where they laid Him.* Mark 16:7 *But go, tell His disciples —and Peter— that He is going before you into Galilee; there you will see Him, as He said to you."*	stood by them in shining garments. Luke 24:5 Then, as they were afraid and bowed their faces to the earth, they said to them, *"Why do you seek the living among the dead?* Luke 24:6 *He is not here, but is risen! Remember how He spoke to you when He was still in Galilee,* Luke 24:7 saying, 'The Son of Man	

	Matthew	Mark	Luke	John
			must be delivered into the hands of sinful men, and be crucified, and the third day rise again.' " Luke 24:8 And they remembered His words.	
Mary Magdalene tells Simon Peter and John that the tomb is empty				John 20:2 Then she ran and came to Simon Peter, and to the other disciple, whom Jesus loved, and said to them, "They have taken away the

	Matthew	Mark	Luke	John
				Lord out of the tomb, and we do not know where they have laid Him."
The other women come to Peter, John and the other disciples and tell them not only of the empty tomb, but also of the angel who declared Christ's resurrecti on (or don't tell	Mat 28:8 So they went out quickly from the tomb with fear and great joy, and ran to bring His disciples word.	Mark 16:8 So they went out quickly and fled from the tomb, for they trembled and were amazed. And they said nothing to anyone, for they were afraid.[33]	Luke 24:9 Then they returned from the tomb and told all these things to the eleven and to all the rest. Luke 24:10 It was Mary Magdalen e, Joanna, Mary the mother of James, and the	

---

[33] According to Matthew Henry, "anyone" refers only to those along the way. However, they carried out the angel's command to tell the disciples. According to Peter Ballard, Mark 16:8 only tells what happened initially and, in any case, the original ending of Mark contained in 16:9--20, which may have written that the women later told the disciples, has been lost.

	Matthew	Mark	Luke	John
anyone)			other women with them, who told these things to the apostles. Luke 24:11 And their words seemed to them like idle tales, and they did not believe them.	
Peter (or Peter and John?) go to the tomb			Luke 24:12 But Peter arose and ran to the tomb; and stooping down, he saw the linen cloths lying by themselves; and he departed,	John 20:3 Peter therefore went out, and the other disciple, and were going to the tomb. John 20:4 So they both ran together, and the

	Matthew	Mark	Luke	John
			marveling to himself at what had happened.	other disciple outran Peter and came to the tomb first.
				John 20:5 And he, stooping down and looking in, saw the linen cloths lying there; yet he did not go in.
				John 20:6 Then Simon Peter came, following him, and went into the tomb; and he saw the linen cloths lying there,
				John 20:7

	Matthew	Mark	Luke	John
				and the handkerchief that had been around His head, not lying with the linen cloths, but folded together in a place by itself. John 20:8 Then the other disciple, who came to the tomb first, went in also; and he saw and believed. John 20:9 For as yet they did not know the Scripture, that He must rise again from the dead.

	Matthew	Mark	Luke	John
				John 20:10 Then the disciples went away again to their own homes.
Mary returns to the tomb a second time and sees the two angels				John 20:11 But Mary stood outside by the tomb weeping, and as she wept she stooped down and looked into the tomb. John 20:12 And she saw two angels in white sitting, one at the head and the other at the feet, where the body of Jesus had lain.

	Matthew	Mark	Luke	John
				John 20:13 Then they said to her, "Woman, why are you weeping?" She said to them, "Because they have taken away my Lord, and I do not know where they have laid Him."
Jesus reveals himself to Mary (Mar, Joh) [or to the women (Mat)].	Mat 28:9 **And as they went to tell His disciples [or simply, "suddenly"], behold, Jesus met them, saying, "Rejoice!" So they came and held Him**	Mark 16:9 Now when He rose early on the first day of the week, He appeared first to Mary Magdalene, out of whom He had cast		John 20:14 Now when she had said this, she turned around and saw Jesus standing there, and did not know that it was Jesus. John 20:15

	Matthew	Mark	Luke	John
	by the feet and worshiped Him. Mat 28:10 Then Jesus said to them, "Do not be afraid. Go and tell My brethren to go to Galilee, and there they will see Me."	seven demons.		Jesus said to her, "Woman, why are you weeping? Whom are you seeking?" She, supposing Him to be the gardener, said to Him, "Sir, if You have carried Him away, tell me where You have laid Him, and I will take Him away." John 20:16 Jesus said to her, "Mary!" She turned and said to Him,

	Matthew	Mark	Luke	John
				"Rabboni! " (which is to say, Teacher). John 20:17 Jesus said to her, "Do not cling to Me, for I have not yet ascended to My Father; but go to My brethren and say to them, 'I am ascending to My Father and your Father, and to My God and your God.' "
Mary tells the disciples what Jesus told her		Mark 16:10 She went and told those who had been with		John 20:18 Mary Magdalene came and told the disciples

	Matthew	Mark	Luke	John
		Him, as they mourned and wept. Mark 16:11 And when they heard that He was alive and had been seen by her, they did not believe.		that she had seen the Lord, and that He had spoken these things to her.
Jesus appears to others		Mark 16:12 After that, He appeared in another form to two of them as they walked and went into the country. Mark 16:13 And they went and		

		Matthew	Mark	Luke	John
			told it to the rest, but they did not believe them either. Mark 16:14 Later He appeared to the eleven as they sat at the table; and He rebuked their unbelief and hardness of heart, because they did not believe those who had seen Him after He had risen. Mark 16:15 And He		

	Matthew	Mark	Luke	John
		said to them, "Go into all the world and preach the gospel to every creature. Mark 16:16 He who believes and is baptized will be saved; but he who does not believe will be condemned. Mark 16:17 And these signs will follow those who believe: In My name they will cast out		

	Matthew	Mark	Luke	John
		demons; they will speak with new tongues;		
		Mark 16:18 they will take up serpents; and if they drink anything deadly, it will by no means hurt them; they will lay hands on the sick, and they will recover."		

2. Revised Synchronization (2018)

Contradictions are underlined in the following synchronization.

Summary	Matthew	Mark	Luke	John
The following women came to see the tomb: John: Mary Magdalene (and implicitly, other women, as Mary Magdalene states "we" in John 20:20) Matthew: Mary Magdalene and Mary the mother of James Mark: Mary	Mat 28:1 Now after the Sabbath, as the first day of the week began to dawn, Mary Magdalene and the other Mary came to see the tomb.	Mark 16:1 Now when the Sabbath was past, Mary Magdalene, Mary the mother of James, and Salome bought spices, that they might come and anoint Him. Mark 16:2 Very early in the morning, on the first day of the	Luke 24:1 Now on the first day of the week, very early in the morning, they, and certain other women with them, came to the tomb bringing the spices which they had prepared.	John 20:1 Now the first day of the week Mary Magdalene went to the tomb early, <u>while it was still dark</u>, and saw that the stone had been taken away from the tomb.

Summary	Matthew	Mark	Luke	John
Magdalene, Mary the mother of James and Salome Luke: at least 5 women (Mary Magdalene, Mary the mother of James, Joanna and "other women") (see verse 24:10)		week, they came to the tomb when the sun had risen.		
Mary Magdalen ran and came to Simon Peter and John and said they have taken				John 20:2 Then she ran and came to Simon Peter, and to the other disciple,

Summary	Matthew	Mark	Luke	John
Jesus from the tomb.				whom Jesus loved, and said to them, "They have taken away the Lord out of the tomb, and we[34] do not know where they have laid Him."
There was an earthquake	Mat 28:2 And behold, there was a great earthquake;			

---

[34] The use of the word "we" implies that Mary was not alone when she came to the tomb. This would be consistent with the accounts in Matthew, Mark and Luke.

Summary	Matthew	Mark	Luke	John
An angel rolled back the stone from the door	for an angel of the Lord descended from heaven, and came and rolled back the stone from the door, and sat on it. Mat 28:3 His countenance was like lightning, and his clothing as white as snow. Mat 28:4 And the guards shook for fear of him,	Mark 16:3 And they said among themselves, "Who will roll away the stone from the door of the tomb for us?" Mark 16:4 But when they looked up, they saw that the stone had been rolled away— for it was very large.	Luke 24:2 But they found the stone rolled away from the tomb.	

Summary	Matthew	Mark	Luke	John
	and became like dead men.			
		Mark 16:5 And entering the tomb, they saw a young man clothed in a long white robe sitting on the right side; and they were alarmed.		
The women did not find Jesus' body.			Luke 24:3 Then they went in and did not find the body of the Lord Jesus.	
According to			Luke 24:4 And it	John 20:11

Summary	Matthew	Mark	Luke	John
Luke, two "men" in shining garments said to the women, "Why do you seek the living among the dead?" According to John, two "angels" sitting in the tomb said to Mary Magdalene, "Woman, why are you weeping?"			happened, as they were greatly perplexed about this, that behold, two men stood by them in shining garments. Luke 24:5 Then, as they were afraid and bowed their faces to the earth, they said to them, "Why do you seek the living among the dead?	But Mary stood outside by the tomb weeping, and as she wept she stooped down and looked into the tomb. John 20:12 And she saw two angels in white sitting, one at the head and the other at the feet, where the body of Jesus had lain. John

Summary	Matthew	Mark	Luke	John
				20:13 Then they said to her, "Woman, why are you weeping?" She said to them, "Because they have taken away my Lord, and I do not know where they have laid Him."
The angel (according to Matthew and Mark; according to Luke,	Mat 28:5 But the angel answered and said to the women, "Do not	Mark 16:6 But he said to them, "Do not be alarmed. You seek Jesus of Nazareth, who was	Luke 24:6 He is not here, but is risen! Remember how He spoke to you when He was still in	

Summary	Matthew	Mark	Luke	John
two men) said to the women not to be afraid and that Jesus rose from the dead.	be afraid, for I know that you seek Jesus who was crucified. Mat 28:6 He is not here; for He is risen, as He said. Come, see the place where the Lord lay.	crucified. He is risen! He is not here. See the place where they laid Him.	Galilee,	
			Luke 24:7 saying, 'The Son of Man must be delivered into the hands of sinful men, and	

Summary	Matthew	Mark	Luke	John
			be crucified, and the third day rise again.' " Luke 24:8 And they remembered His words.	
The angel told the women: - to tell the disciples that Jesus is risen. - That He is going before them to Galilee - That they will see Him there	Mat 28:7 And go quickly and tell His disciples that He is risen from the dead, and indeed He is going before you into Galilee; there you will see Him. Behold,	Mark 16:7 But go, tell His disciples —and Peter— that He is going before you into Galilee; there you will see Him, as He said to you."		

Summary	Matthew	Mark	Luke	John
	I have told you."			
The women ran from the tomb to bring His disciples word that the tomb was empty.	Mat 28:8 So they went out quickly from the tomb with fear and great joy, and ran to bring His disciples word.		Luke 24:9 Then they returned from the tomb and told all these things to the eleven and to all the rest. Luke 24:10 It was Mary Magdalene, Joanna, Mary the mother of James, and the other women with them, who told these things to the apostles.	[John 20:2 Then she ran and came to Simon Peter, and to the other disciple, whom Jesus loved, and said to them, "They have taken away the Lord out of the tomb, and we do not know where they have laid Him."]

Summary	Matthew	Mark	Luke	John
The women <u>did not</u> bring the disciples word, for they were afraid.		Mark 16:8 So they went out quickly and fled from the tomb, for they trembled and were amazed. And they said nothing to anyone, for they were afraid.		
Jesus met the women and told them to go and tell his disciples to go to Galilee, or, alternatively:	Mat 28:9 And as they went to tell His disciples, behold, Jesus met them, saying, "Rejoice!" So they			

Summary	Matthew	Mark	Luke	John
	came and held Him by the feet and worshiped Him. Mat 28:10 Then Jesus said to them, "Do not be afraid. Go and tell My brethren to go to Galilee, and there they will see Me."			
Jesus appeared first to Mary Magdalene. According to		Mark 16:9 Now when He rose early on the first day of the week, He		John 20:14 Now when she had said this, she turned around

Summary	Matthew	Mark	Luke	John
John, Jesus asked Mary Magdalene why she was weeping. She thought Jesus was the gardener, but then her eyes were opened.		appeared first to Mary Magdalene, out of whom He had cast seven demons.		and saw Jesus standing there, and did not know that it was Jesus. John 20:15 Jesus said to her, "Woman, why are you weeping? Whom are you seeking?" She, supposing Him to be the gardener, said to Him, "Sir, if You have carried Him

Summary	Matthew	Mark	Luke	John
				away, tell me where You have laid Him, and I will take Him away." John 20:16 Jesus said to her, "Mary!" She turned and said to Him, "Rabboni!" (which is to say, Teacher). John 20:17 Jesus said to her, "Do not cling to Me, for I

Summary	Matthew	Mark	Luke	John
				have not yet ascended to My Father; but go to My brethren and say to them, 'I am ascending to My Father and your Father, and to My God and your God.' "
Mary Magdalene went and told the disciples		Mark 16:10 She went and told those who had been with Him, as they mourned and wept.		John 20:18 Mary Magdalene came and told the disciples that she had seen the Lord, and that He had

Summary	Matthew	Mark	Luke	John
				spoken these things to her.
The disciples did not believe Mary (according to Mark, or, according to Luke, the women).		Mark 16:11 And when they heard that He was alive and had been seen by her, they did not believe.	Luke 24:11 And their words seemed to them like idle tales, and they did not believe them.	
The guards reported to the chief priests the things that had happened. The chief priests assembled with the elders	Mat 28:11 Now while they were going, behold, some of the guard came into the city and reported to the chief			

Summary	Matthew	Mark	Luke	John
and gave the soldiers money and instructed them to say the disciples stole the body while they slept.	priests all the things that had happened. Mat 28:12 When they had assembled with the elders and consulted together, they gave a large sum of money to the soldiers, Mat 28:13 saying, "Tell them, 'His disciples came at			

Summary	Matthew	Mark	Luke	John
	night and stole Him away while we slept.' Mat 28:14 And if this comes to the governor's ears, we will appease him and make you secure." Mat 28:15 So they took the money and did as they were instructed; and this saying is			

Summary	Matthew	Mark	Luke	John
	commonly reported among the Jews until this day.			
Peter [and, according to John, the "other disciple"] went to the tomb and saw the linen cloths.			Luke 24:12 But Peter arose and ran to the tomb; and stooping down, he saw the linen cloths lying by themselves; and he departed, marveling to himself at what had happened.	John 20:3 Peter therefore went out, and the other disciple, and were going to the tomb. John 20:4 So they both ran together, and the other disciple outran Peter and came to the tomb first. John 20:5 And

Summary	Matthew	Mark	Luke	John
				he, stooping down and looking in, saw the linen cloths lying there; yet he did not go in. John 20:6 Then Simon Peter came, following him, and went into the tomb; and he saw the linen cloths lying there, John 20:7 and the

Summary	Matthew	Mark	Luke	John
				handkerchief that had been around His head, not lying with the linen cloths, but folded together in a place by itself. John 20:8 Then the other disciple, who came to the tomb first, went in also; and he saw and believed. John 20:9 For as yet they did

Summary	Matthew	Mark	Luke	John
				not know the Scripture, that He must rise again from the dead. John 20:10 Then the disciples went away again to their own homes.
Jesus appeared to two disciples.		Mark 16:12 After that, He appeared in another form to two of them as they walked and went into the country.	Luke 24:13 Now behold, two of them were traveling that same day to a village called Emmaus, which was seven miles	

Summary	Matthew	Mark	Luke	John
			from Jerusalem. Luke 24:14 And they talked together of all these things which had happened. Luke 24:15 So it was, while they conversed and reasoned, that Jesus Himself drew near and went with them.	
After conversing with Him, they invited Him to stay with them.			Luke 24:16 But their eyes were restrained, so that they did not know	

Summary	Matthew	Mark	Luke	John
After he broke bread with them, their eyes were opened and they knew Him.			Him. Luke 24:17 And He said to them, "What kind of conversation is this that you have with one another as you walk and are sad?" Luke 24:18 Then the one whose name was Cleopas answered and said to Him, "Are You the only stranger in Jerusalem, and have You not known the things	

Summary	Matthew	Mark	Luke	John
			which happened there in these days?" Luke 24:19 And He said to them, "What things?" So they said to Him, "The things concerning Jesus of Nazareth, who was a Prophet mighty in deed and word before God and all the people, Luke 24:20 and how the chief priests and our	

Summary	Matthew	Mark	Luke	John
			rulers delivered Him to be condemned to death, and crucified Him. Luke 24:21 But we were hoping that it was He who was going to redeem Israel. Indeed, besides all this, today is the third day since these things happened. Luke 24:22 Yes, and certain women of our company, who	

Summary	Matthew	Mark	Luke	John
			arrived at the tomb early, astonished us. Luke 24:23 When they did not find His body, they came saying that they had also seen a vision of angels who said He was alive. Luke 24:24 And certain of those who were with us went to the tomb and found it just as the women had said;	

Summary	Matthew	Mark	Luke	John
			but Him they did not see." Luke 24:25 Then He said to them, "O foolish ones, and slow of heart to believe in all that the prophets have spoken! Luke 24:26 Ought not the Christ to have suffered these things and to enter into His glory?" Luke 24:27 And beginning at Moses and all the	

Summary	Matthew	Mark	Luke	John
			Prophets, He expounded to them in all the Scriptures the things concerning Himself. Luke 24:28 Then they drew near to the village where they were going, and He indicated that He would have gone farther. Luke 24:29 But they constrained Him, saying, "Abide with us, for it is	

Summary	Matthew	Mark	Luke	John
			toward evening, and the day is far spent." And He went in to stay with them.	
			Luke 24:30 Now it came to pass, as He sat at the table with them, that He took bread, blessed and broke it, and gave it to them.	
			Luke 24:31 Then their eyes were opened and they knew Him; and	

Summary	Matthew	Mark	Luke	John
			He vanished from their sight. Luke 24:32 And they said to one another, "Did not our heart burn within us while He talked with us on the road, and while He opened the Scriptures to us?"	
According to Mark, the two disciples told the others, but they did not believe		Mark 16:13 And they went and told it to the rest, but they did not believe them	Luke 24:33 So they rose up that very hour and returned to Jerusalem, and found	

Summary	Matthew	Mark	Luke	John
them. According to Luke, the two disciples went to the 11 Apostles, who said Jesus rose and appeared to Simon.[35]		either.	the eleven and those who were with them gathered together, Luke 24:34 saying, "The Lord is risen indeed, and has appeared to Simon!" Luke 24:35 And they told about the things that had happened on the road, and how He was known to them in	

[35] This would be a contradiction if the "others" referenced in Mark are the 11 Apostles referenced in Luke. The "others" would not be a state of disbelief if they said "The Lord is risen indeed."

Summary	Matthew	Mark	Luke	John
			the breaking of bread.	
Jesus stood in the midst of the Apostles. They did not believe because of joy and marvel. They gave him broiled fish and a honeycomb and he ate.			Luke 24:36 Now as they said these things, Jesus Himself stood in the midst of them, and said to them, "Peace to you." Luke 24:37 But they were terrified and frightened, and supposed they had seen a spirit. Luke 24:38 And He said to them,	

Summary	Matthew	Mark	Luke	John
			"Why are you troubled? And why do doubts arise in your hearts? Luke 24:39 Behold My hands and My feet, that it is I Myself. Handle Me and see, for a spirit does not have flesh and bones as you see I have." Luke 24:40 When He had said this, He showed them His hands and	

Summary	Matthew	Mark	Luke	John
			His feet. Luke 24:41 But while they still did not believe for joy, and marveled, He said to them, "Have you any food here?" Luke 24:42 So they gave Him a piece of a broiled fish and some honeycomb. Luke 24:43 And He took it and ate in their presence.	
Jesus			Luke	

Summary	Matthew	Mark	Luke	John
told the Apostles and disciples that the words of the prophets had to be fulfilled and He commanded them to remain in Jerusalem until they have received power from heaven.			24:44 Then He said to them, "These are the words which I spoke to you while I was still with you, that all things must be fulfilled which were written in the Law of Moses and the Prophets and the Psalms concerning Me." Luke 24:45 And He opened their understanding, that	

Summary	Matthew	Mark	Luke	John
			they might comprehend the Scriptures. Luke 24:46 Then He said to them, "Thus it is written, and thus it was necessary for the Christ to suffer and to rise from the dead the third day, Luke 24:47 and that repentance and remission of sins should be preached in His	

Summary	Matthew	Mark	Luke	John
			name to all nations, beginning at Jerusalem. Luke 24:48 And you are witnesses of these things. Luke 24:49 Behold, I send the Promise of My Father upon you; but tarry in the city of Jerusalem until you are endued with power from on high."	
The 11 disciples	Mat 28:16	Mark 16:14		John 20:19

Summary	Matthew	Mark	Luke	John
saw Jesus. They worshipped him, but some did not believe (Matthew); Jesus rebuked their unbelief (Mark).	Then the eleven disciples went away into Galilee, to the mountain which Jesus had appointed for them. Mat 28:17 When they saw Him, they worshiped Him; but some doubted.	Later He appeared to the eleven as they sat at the table; and He rebuked their unbelief and hardness of heart, because they did not believe those who had seen Him after He had risen.		Then, the same day at evening, being the first day of the week, when the doors were shut where the disciples were assembled, for fear of the Jews, Jesus came and stood in the midst, and said to them, "Peace be with you."
Jesus showed				John 20:20

Summary	Matthew	Mark	Luke	John
the disciples his hands and his side, gave them the Holy Spirit and told them that they had power to forgive sins				When He had said this, He showed them His hands and His side. Then the disciples were glad when they saw the Lord. t John 20:21 So Jesus said to them again, "Peace to you! As the Father has sent Me, I also send you." John 20:22 And

Summary	Matthew	Mark	Luke	John
				when He had said this, He breathed on them, and said to them, "Receive the Holy Spirit. John 20:23 If you forgive the sins of any, they are forgiven them; if you retain the sins of any, they are retained. "
Jesus shows himself to Thomas.				John 20:24 Now Thomas, called the Twin,

Summary	Matthew	Mark	Luke	John
				one of the twelve, was not with them when Jesus came. John 20:25 The other disciples therefore said to him, "We have seen the Lord." So he said to them, "Unless I see in His hands the print of the nails, and put my

Summary	Matthew	Mark	Luke	John
				finger into the print of the nails, and put my hand into His side, I will not believe." John 20:26 And after eight days His disciples were again inside, and Thomas with them. Jesus came, the doors being shut, and stood in the midst, and said,

Summary	Matthew	Mark	Luke	John
				"Peace to you!" John 20:27 Then He said to Thomas, "Reach your finger here, and look at My hands; and reach your hand here, and put it into My side. Do not be unbelieving, but believing." John 20:28 And Thomas answered and said

Summary	Matthew	Mark	Luke	John
				to Him, "My Lord and my God!" John 20:29 Jesus said to him, "Thomas, because you have seen Me, you have believed. Blessed are those who have not seen and yet have believed."
Jesus commanded the apostles to make disciples of the nations.	Mat 28:18 And Jesus came and spoke to them, saying,	Mark 16:15 And He said to them, "Go into all the world and preach the		

Summary	Matthew	Mark	Luke	John
	"All authority has been given to Me in heaven and on earth. Mat 28:19 Go therefore and make disciples of all the nations, baptizing them in the name of the Father and of the Son and of the Holy Spirit, Mat 28:20 teaching them to observe	gospel to every creature. Mark 16:16 He who believes and is baptized will be saved; but he who does not believe will be condemned.		

Summary	Matthew	Mark	Luke	John
	all things that I have commanded you; and lo, I am with you always, even to the end of the age." Amen.			
Jesus spoke of the signs that will come: casting out of demons, speaking in tongues, immunity from poison and healing.		Mark 16:17 And these signs will follow those who believe: In My name they will cast out demons; they will speak with new tongues; Mark 16:18		

Summary	Matthew	Mark	Luke	John
		they will take up serpents; and if they drink anything deadly, it will by no means hurt them; they will lay hands on the sick, and they will recover."		
Jesus ascended into heaven.		Mark 16:19 So then, after the Lord had spoken to them, He was received up into heaven, and sat down at the right hand of God.	Luke 24:50 And He led them out as far as Bethany, and He lifted up His hands and blessed them. Luke 24:51 Now it came to pass,	

Summary	Matthew	Mark	Luke	John
			while He blessed them, that He was parted from them and carried up into heaven. Luke 24:52 And they worshiped Him, and returned to Jerusalem with great joy, Luke 24:53 and were continually in the temple praising and blessing God. Amen.	
The disciples		Mark 16:20		

Summary	Matthew	Mark	Luke	John
preached the good news.		And they went out and preached everywhere, the Lord working with them and confirming the word through the accompanying signs. Amen.		

III. WHETHER JESUS WAS IN THE HEART OF THE EARTH THREE DAYS AND THREE NIGHTS

1. Overview

Mat 12:40 For as Jonah was three days and three nights in the belly of the great fish, so will the <u>Son of Man be three days and three nights in the heart of the earth.</u>

The Scriptures state that Jesus was crucified on Friday and was taken to the tomb *late that evening*, as the Sabbath was approaching:

> Mat 27:57 Now *when evening had come*, there came a
> rich man from Arimathea, named Joseph, who himself
> had also become a disciple of Jesus.
> Mark 15:42 Now *when evening had come*, because it
> was the Preparation Day, that is, the day before the
> Sabbath
> Luke 23:53 Then [Joseph] took [Jesus' body] down,
> wrapped it in linen, and laid it in a tomb that was hewn
> out of the rock, where no one had ever lain before.
> Luke 23:54 That day was the Preparation, and *the
> Sabbath drew near.*

Therefore, Jesus was not in the tomb during the day
on Friday; he entered the tomb that evening.

The Scriptures then state that while it was still dark on
Sunday morning, Jesus was no longer in the tomb:

> John 20:1 Now the first day of the week Mary
> Magdalene went to the tomb early, while it was still
> dark, and saw that the stone had been taken away from
> the tomb.

Therefore, the only *day* (excluding nights) that Jesus
had been in the tomb was Saturday (one day) and,
possibly, a few minutes on Friday just before sundown.

2. Proposed Explanation 1: Jesus Was Crucified on a Wednesday

a. Overview

A second explanation as to the issue of there not being
three days between Thursday evening and Sunday
morning is that two Sabbaths are discussed in the
Scripture: one—the weekly (Saturday) Sabbath, and the
second, an annual feast day Sabbath that fell on a
Thursday. According to the United Church of God, this
explanation aligns with various characteristics of the
descriptions given in the Scripture. It holds as follows:

- Jesus was arrested at Gethsemane on Tuesday night;
- On Wednesday night, on the eve of an annual feast day Sabbath that fell on a Thursday, Jesus was crucified and placed in the tomb.
- Jesus remained in the tomb:
  o On the evenings of Wednesday, Thursday and Friday (three nights).
  o On Thursday, Friday and Saturday (three days).
- Jesus rose from the dead just before sunset on Saturday.
- When Mary came to the tomb on Sunday morning, Christ had already risen from the dead about 12 hours earlier, the night before.

b. Problem with Proposed Explanation

If Jesus was in fact crucified on a Wednesday night rather than on a Friday night and rose on Saturday before sunset rather than on Sunday, then approximately two thousand years of church history would have somehow and inexplicably gotten these fundamental facts wrong, which in itself is difficult to lend credence to.

3. Proposed Explanation 2: "Clutches of the Earth" Theory

a. Overview

As a possible explanation, Pastor Doug from AmazingFacts.org argues that the "heart of the earth" is not the tomb, but rather, the "clutches" of the earth[36]:

---

[36]   See   <https://www.amazingfacts.org/media-library/media/e/1170/f/6/t/explain-how-jesus-was-in-the-tomb-3-days-/-3-nights->.

There is a major misconception here regarding the heart of the earth. Everyone assumes that means the tomb, yet <u>nowhere else in the Bible is the heart of the earth called the tomb</u>. For instance, in Matthew, when we say the Lord's Prayer, "Thy will be done, in earth, as it is in Heaven," this does not mean Thy will be done in the tomb.

When Jesus alluded to three days and three nights in the heart of the earth, He wasn't talking about the tomb or vault. Rather, He was referring to the heart of the earth, or the "clutches" of the world. Every time the mob tried to destroy Jesus or stone Jesus or throw Him off a cliff during his earthly ministry, He walked right through their midst. They never were able to harm Him because He was under His Father's protection. But on Thursday night in the Garden of Gethsemane, when He said quite specifically, "Now is the hour of darkness," He was tied up, beat, and began suffering for the sins of the world.

He didn't start suffering for the sins of the world when He was on the Cross and the nails pierced His flesh. The suffering began in the Garden of Gethsemane, where He was taken from place to place and beaten and mobbed. He went from Pilate to Herod and back to Pilate again; from Caiaphas to Anna and back to Caiaphas. He was dragged from one place to another and mocked and whipped and had thorns placed on His head. He was suffering for the sins of the world. He was a captive to the devil the same way Jonah went wherever the whale went. Jonah was a captive to the whale for three days and three nights the same way that Jesus was in the clutches of the lost world, for three days and three nights.

b. First Problem

a. *Overview*

A problem with this explanation is it only explains how Jesus could be in the "heart of the earth" for two days (Friday and Saturday) and three nights (Thursday, Friday, and Saturday).

b. Response: The Use of Inclusive Reckoning

The counting of time known as "inclusive reckoning," which counts any part of any day as a full day (as discussed by Amazingfacts.org), can explain the discrepancy. Jesus makes this simple way of counting time crystal clear in Luke 13:32-33:

> Luke 13:32 And He said to them, "Go, tell that fox, 'Behold, I cast out demons and perform cures today and tomorrow, and the third day I shall be perfected.' Luke 13:33 Nevertheless I must journey today, tomorrow, and the day following; for it cannot be that a prophet should perish outside of Jerusalem.

Here, "today" is the first day, "tomorrow" is the second day, and the day after tomorrow is the third day.

Therefore, Jesus was in the "heart of the earth" for three nights (the Thursday of his arrest at Gethsamene, the Friday of his crucifixion at Golgotha and the Saturday in the tomb prior to his resurrection) and three days, as follows:

- Friday (during the day) = Day 1
- Saturday (Jesus rested) = Day 2
- Sunday (the evening between Saturday and Sunday and Sunday morning) = Day 3

In order to accept this interpretation, one must recognize that under the system of biblical inclusive reckoning, any part of one day is counted as the whole day. The NIV Bible makes this point at the Matthew 12:40 text note, which states:

Three days and three nights. Including at least part of
the first day and part of the third day, a common
Jewish reckoning of time.

c. Second Problem

The second problem with the Proposed Explanation is
that Jesus Says He Will Be in the "Heart of the Earth,"
not "on Earth," for Three Days and Three Nights. Pastor
Doug from AmazingFacts.org writes the following with
respect to the "clutches of the earth" theory[37]:

> There is a major misconception here regarding the
> heart of the earth. Everyone assumes that means the
> tomb, yet nowhere else in the Bible is the heart of the
> earth called the tomb. For instance, in Matthew, when
> we say the Lord's Prayer, "Thy will be done, in earth,
> as it is in Heaven," this does not mean Thy will be
> done in the tomb.

It is true that "nowhere else in the Bible is the heart of
the earth called the tomb." But it is also true that "heart of
the earth" is found nowhere in the Bible other than in
Matthew 12:40. Therefore, it is inappropriate and
inapropos to compare the language "in the heart of the
earth" with other references to the "earth," such as the
reference to "on earth as it is in heaven" in the Lord's
prayer at Matthew 6:10, which do not match Jesus'
language in Matthew 12:40.

Moreover, it is important to point out that Jesus did
not say that he would be three days and three nights in the
"clutches of the earth," which could be interpreted to
mean the clutches of the world. Rather, he said he would
be in the "heart of the earth." Comparing this language to

---

[37]   See   <https://www.amazingfacts.org/media-
library/media/e/1170/f/6/t/explain-how-jesus-was-in-the-tomb-3-
days-/-3-nights->.

the language "on earth" in the Lord's prayer is problematic. The Lord's prayer simply states "thy will be done on earth," not "thy will be done in the heart of the earth." Therefore, we should not compare His words at Matthew 12:40 with his words at Matthew 6:10, because they are different.

Rather, we should come to understand what Jesus meant by "heart of the earth" by looking to the context. Most likely, He was referring to the tomb. This is made clear by the prophecies of Jesus dying and rising from the dead, including:

> Mat 16:21 From that time Jesus began to show to His disciples that He must go to Jerusalem, and suffer many things from the elders and chief priests and scribes, and be killed, and be raised the third day.
>
> Mat 17:22 Now while they were staying in Galilee, Jesus said to them, "The Son of Man is about to be betrayed into the hands of men, Mat 17:23 and they will kill Him, and the third day He will be raised up."
>
> Mat 20:18 "Behold, we are going up to Jerusalem, and the Son of Man will be betrayed to the chief priests and to the scribes; and they will condemn Him to death, Mat 20:19 and deliver Him to the Gentiles to mock and to scourge and to crucify. And the third day He will rise again."
>
> Mat 27:62 On the next day, which followed the Day of Preparation, the chief priests and Pharisees gathered together to Pilate, Mat 27:63 saying, "Sir, we remember, while He was still alive, how that deceiver said, 'After three days I will rise.' Mat 27:64 Therefore command that the tomb be made secure until the third day, lest His disciples come by night and steal Him away, and say to the people, 'He has risen from the dead.' So the last deception will be worse than the first."
>
> Luke 24:46 Then He said to them, "Thus it is written, and thus it was necessary for the Christ to suffer and to rise from the dead the third day,

In predicting His death, in contrast, Jesus specifically states that he will be "in the heart of the earth." To argue that by "heart of the earth," Jesus means anything but a tomb would be improbable.

4. Proposed Explanation 3: Jesus was in the Tomb Three Days and Two Nights, but Hebrew Idioms Evenly Pair Days and Nights

Under this explanation, Jesus was in the tomb three days and two nights, but due to the structure of the Hebrew language and the use of idioms, the nights were paired with the days to reach three days and two nights.[38] A Jew at the time of Jesus' prediction would never state, "three days and two nights." Indeed, you can search all of scripture and never find days and nights unevenly paired. Consider:

- Gen 7:4 For after seven more days I will cause it to rain on the earth forty days and forty nights, and I will destroy from the face of the earth all living things that I have made."
- Gen 7:12 And the rain was on the earth forty days and forty nights.
- Exo 24:18 So Moses went into the midst of the cloud and went up into the mountain. And Moses was on the mountain forty days and forty nights.
- Exo 34:28 So he was there with the Lord forty days and forty nights; he neither ate bread nor drank water. And He wrote on the tablets the words of the covenant, the Ten Commandments.
- Deu 9:9 When I went up into the mountain to receive the tablets of stone, the tablets of the

---

[38] This explanation was proferred by Reagan Kollmar on 8 Sept. 2018.

covenant which the Lord made with you, then I stayed on the mountain forty days and forty nights. I neither ate bread nor drank water.

- Deu 9:11 And it came to pass, at the end of forty days and forty nights, that the Lord gave me the two tablets of stone, the tablets of the covenant.
- Deu 9:18 And I fell down before the Lord, as at the first, forty days and forty nights; I neither ate bread nor drank water, because of all your sin which you committed in doing wickedly in the sight of the Lord, to provoke Him to anger.
- Deu 9:25 "Thus I prostrated myself before the Lord; forty days and forty nights I kept prostrating myself, because the Lord had said He would destroy you.
- Deu 10:10 "As at the first time, I stayed in the mountain forty days and forty nights; the Lord also heard me at that time, and the Lord chose not to destroy you.
- 1Sa 30:12 And they gave him a piece of a cake of figs and two clusters of raisins. So when he had eaten, his strength came back to him; for he had eaten no bread nor drunk water for three days and three nights.
- 1Sa 30:12 And they gave him a piece of a cake of figs and two clusters of raisins. So when he had eaten, his strength came back to him; for he had eaten no bread nor drunk water for three days and three nights.
- 1Ki 19:8 So he arose, and ate and drank; and he went in the strength of that food forty days and forty nights as far as Horeb, the mountain of God.
- Job 2:13 So they sat down with him on the ground seven days and seven nights, and no one spoke a word to him, for they saw that his grief was very great.

- Jon 1:17 Now the Lord had prepared a great fish to swallow Jonah. And Jonah was in the belly of the fish three days and three nights.
- Mat 4:2 And when He had fasted forty days and forty nights, afterward He was hungry.
- Mat 12:40 For as Jonah was three days and three nights in the belly of the great fish, so will the Son of Man be three days and three nights in the heart of the earth.

Therefore, according to the use of Jewish idioms and the general use of the Hebrew language, any part of a day is counted as a full day (i.e., as a day and a night), even if only a portion of the night is included without any daylight or if only a portion of the day is included without any night. In either case, the day is counted as a full day and a full night.

In other words, whether an event lasts for 24 seconds or 24 hours, it is counted as "one day and one night" in the Hebrew language as it was used in biblical times. This is seen in countless examples of paired days and nights used throughout the Scriptures.

IV. HOW MANY MARY'S THERE WERE

1. Overview

a. Mary is Accompanied in Matthew, Mark and Luke

Mat 28:1 Now after the Sabbath, as the first day of the week began to dawn, Mary Magdalene and the other Mary came to see the tomb.

Mark 16:1 Now when the Sabbath was past, Mary Magdalene, Mary the mother of James, and Salome bought spices.

Luke 24:1 Now on the first day of the week, very early in the morning, they, and certain other women with them, came to the tomb bringing the spices which they had prepared … Luke 24:10 It was <u>Mary Magdalene, Joanna, Mary the mother of James, and the other women with them</u>, who told these things to the apostles.

b. Mary is Alone in John

John 20:1 Now the first day of the week <u>Mary Magdalene went to the tomb early</u>, while it was still dark, and saw that the stone had been taken away from the tomb.

2. Explanation

The discrepant accounts of how many Mary's visited the tomb are not necessarily contradictions. Most likely, there were several women who were present at the tomb, but not all of the accounts provide full details as to all of the women that were present. This does not necessarily mean that the Gospel authors are contradicting each other. If Alpha, Bravo and Charlie were all present at a dinner, but A states that Alpha and Bravo were present and B states that Bravo and Charlie were present, then it is possible that all three could have been present at the same dinner, provided A and B did not state that "only" Alpha and Bravo or "only" Bravo and Charlie were present. None of the Gospel writers state that "only" the women they recount were present, so it is possible that more than those recounted were present.

Moreover, John likely recognized that Mary Magdalene was accompanied by other women when she visited the tomb, as he recounts her as stating "They have taken away the Lord out of the tomb, and <u>we</u> do not know where they have laid Him" in John 20:2. If she had not been accompanied, she would not have stated "we."

Most likely, the following women came to see the tomb together:

- Mary Magdalene (according to Matthew, Mark, Luke and John)
- Mary the mother of James (according to Matthew, Mark and Luke)
- Salome (Mark)
- Joanna and other women (Luke)

V. WHEN MARY MAGDALENE ARRIVED TO THE TOMB

1. Overview

a. Matthew, Mark and Luke: She Arrived at the First Dawn / Early in the Morning

According to Matthew, Mark and Luke, Mary Magdalene arrived to the tomb when the first day started to dawn / very early in the morning:

> Mat 28:1 Now after the Sabbath, <u>as the first day of the week began to dawn</u>, Mary Magdalene and the other Mary came to see the tomb.
> Mark 16:1 Now when the Sabbath was past, Mary Magdalene, Mary the mother of James, and Salome bought spices, that they might come and anoint Him.
> Mark 16:2 <u>Very early in the morning</u>, on the first day of the week, <u>they came to the tomb when the sun had risen</u>.
> Luke 24:1 Now on the first day of the week, <u>very early in the morning</u>, they, and certain other women with them, came to the tomb bringing the spices which they had prepared.

b. John: She Arrived When It was Still Dark

According to John, however, it was when it was still dark when Mary Magdalene went to the tomb:

John 20:1 Now the first day of the week Mary Magdalene <u>went</u> to the tomb early, <u>while it was still dark</u>, and saw that the stone had been taken away from the tomb.

2. Meaning of ἔρχομαι (G2064 / erchomai)

a. Use of ἔρχομαι (G2064 / erchomai)

All four Gospels use a conjugation of the irregular Greek verb ἔρχομαι (G2064 / erchomai):

- Matthew 28:1 uses ηλθεν (ilthen)
- Mark 16:2 uses ερχονται (erchontai)
- Luke 24:1 uses ηλθον (ilthon)
- John 20:1 uses ερχεται (erchetai)

This is an irregular verb, which is why it looks so different in some forms. The word means to come or go, so it can be translated variously, depending on the context. In Matthew 28:1 and Luke 24:1, the verb is appears in aorist form, which is why it looks so different.

b. Meaning of G2064

ἔρχομαι is defined as:

Strong's G2064 – erchomai / ἔρχομαι / e'r-kho-mī
Part of Speech: verb

According to Strong's Definitions:

ἔρχομαι érchomai, er'-khom-ahee; middle voice of a primary verb (used only in the present and imperfect tenses, the others being supplied by a kindred (middle voice) ἐλεύθομαι eleúthomai el-yoo'-thom-ahee, or (active) ἔλθω élthō el'-tho, which do not otherwise occur); to <u>come or go</u> (in a great variety of applications, literally and figuratively):—accompany, <u>appear</u>, bring, <u>come</u>, <u>enter</u>, fall out, go, grow, × light, × next, pass, resort, be set.

ἔρχομαι (erchomai) could mean to set off or leave (one of the meanings is "go"), but it could also mean to arrive. Most of the definitions (*e.g.*, appear, come, enter) revolve around the idea of arriving.

3. Explanation: Matthew, Mark and Luke Refer to When the Women Arrived; John Refers to When They Set Off to the Tomb

Given the broad range of definitions that can be ascribed to ἔρχομαι (G2064 / erchomai), it is possible that Matthew, Mark and Luke, in employing the term, were referring to the time that Mary Magdalene *arrived* to the tomb, whereas John, using the same terms, was applying the "set off to" or "go" meaning to refer to when Mary Magdalene went to the tomb. Mary Magdalene could have set off for the tomb while it was still dark and arrived there just as it began to dawn.

VI. HOW MANY ANGELS WERE AT THE TOMB

1. Overview

a. Matthew: One Angel of the Lord <u>Sitting</u> on the Stone

According to Matthew, the women encountered <u>an angel of the Lord</u> sitting on the stone:

> Mat 28:2 And behold, there was a *great earthquake*; for <u>an angel of the Lord</u> descended from heaven, and came and rolled back the stone from the door, and sat on it. Mat 28:3 His countenance was like lightning, and his clothing as white as snow. Mat 28:4 And the guards shook for fear of him, and became like dead men. Mat 28:5 But the angel answered and said to the women, "*Do not be afraid, for I know that you seek Jesus who was crucified. Mat 28:6 He is not here; for He is risen, as He said. Come, see the place where the*

> *Lord lay. Mat 28:7 And go quickly and tell His disciples that He is risen from the dead, and indeed He is going before you into Galilee; there you will see Him. Behold, I have told you."*

b. Mark: One Young Man Clothed in a Long White Robe <u>Sitting</u> on the Right Side of the Tomb

According to Mark, the women encountered a <u>young man clothed in a long white robe</u> sitting on the right side of the tomb:

> Mark 16:5 And entering the tomb, they saw a <u>young man clothed in a long white robe</u> sitting on the right side; and they were alarmed. Mark 16:6 But he said to them, *"Do not be alarmed. You seek Jesus of Nazareth, who was crucified. He is risen! He is not here. See the place where they laid Him. Mark 16:7 But go, tell His disciples—and Peter—that He is going before you into Galilee; there you will see Him, as He said to you."*

c. Luke: Two Men <u>Standing</u> by the Women in Shining Garments

According to Luke, the women arrived to the tomb and "found the stone rolled away from the tomb" (Luke 24:2). They went in and did not find the body of the Lord Jesus (Luke 24:3). They then encountered <u>two men standing by them in shining garments</u> (Luke 24:4):

> Luke 24:4 And it happened, as they were greatly perplexed about this, that behold, <u>two men stood by them in shining garments</u>. Luke 24:5 Then, as they were afraid and bowed their faces to the earth, they said to them, *"Why do you seek the living among the dead? Luke 24:6 He is not here, but is risen! Remember how He spoke to you when He was still in Galilee, Luke 24:7 saying, 'The Son of Man must be delivered into the hands of sinful men, and be crucified, and the third day rise again.'"*

d. John: Two Angels in White <u>Sitting</u>, One at the Head and the Other at the Feet

According to John, Mary Magdalene went to the tomb, found it empty and then told Peter and John, who went to inspect it. After Peter and John departed, Mary stood outside by the tomb weeping. As she wept she stooped down and looked into the tomb (John 20:11) and saw <u>two angels in white sitting</u>, one at the head and the other at the feet, where the body of Jesus had lain (John 20:12):

> John 20:12 And she saw <u>two angels in white sitting</u>, one at the head and the other at the feet, where the body of Jesus had lain. John 20:13 Then they said to her, "*Woman, why are you weeping?*" She said to them, "Because they have taken away my Lord, and I do not know where they have laid Him."

2. Attempted Harmonization

a. Matthew and Mark's Account of One Angel
   - According to Matthew, the women encountered <u>an angel of the Lord</u> sitting on the stone (Mat 28:2).
   - According to Mark, the women encountered a <u>young man clothed in a long white robe</u> sitting on the right side of the tomb (Mark 16:5).

Neither Matthew nor Mark state that the women encountered <u>only</u> one angel or <u>only</u> one young man. In fact, they do not even state that the women encountered "one" angel or "one" young man; they simply state that they encountered "an angel" and "a young man." It is entirely possible that there were two angels, one sitting on the stone and another sitting on the right side of the tomb, but Matthew and Mark each gave an account of only one of each of them.

b. Luke and John's Account of Two Angels

According to Luke, the women arrived to the tomb and "found the stone rolled away from the tomb" (Luke 24:2). They went in and did not find the body of the Lord Jesus (Luke 24:3). They then encountered <u>two men standing by them in shining garments</u> (Luke 24:4):

- Luke 24:4 And it happened, as they were greatly perplexed about this, that behold, <u>two men stood by them in shining garments</u>. Luke 24:5 Then, as they were afraid and bowed their faces to the earth, they said to them, "Why do you seek the living among the dead?"

It is possible that one angel descended from heaven, rolled back the stone from the door and sat on it, as recounted by Matthew. Meanwhile, a second angel entered the tomb and sat on the right side, as recounted by Mark. The angels then shifted their positions and stood up, next to the perplexed women, as recounted by Luke, who describes them as "two men who stood by them in shining garments" (Luke 24:4).

According to John, Mary Magdalene went to the tomb, found it empty and then told Peter and John, who went to inspect it. Mary and the other women[39] could have encountered the angel who was sitting on the stone when it was rolled away and the angel sitting inside the tomb when they first came to the empty tomb in John 20:1. The two angels could have then shifted positions, standing up next to the perplexed women, as recounted in Luke 24:4. Mary would have then ran to Peter and John and told them of the empty tomb, as recounted in John 20:2. While she was absent from the tomb, the angels may

---

[39] Mary Magdalene tells Peter and John, "we do not know where they have laid Him" (John 20:2), implying that she was not alone at the time she encountered the empty tomb.

have again shifted positions, moving into the tomb. Therefore, as Mary wept she stooped down and looked into the tomb (John 20:11), she saw the two angels in white sitting, one at the head and the other at the feet, where the body of Jesus had lain (John 20:12).

c. Conclusion

The Evangelists' disparate accounts of the number of angels or men are not necessarily contradictions. One possible explanation is as follows:

- Mary Magdalene went to the tomb, found it empty and then told Peter and John, who went to inspect it (John).
- Mary Magdalene and the other women came to the tomb and saw that the stone had been taken away (John 20:1)
- The women encountered an angel who was sitting on the stone that was rolled away (Mat 28:2). There was great fear and the guards became like dead men (Mat 28:4).
- The angel moved into the tomb [implied] and spoke to the women, telling them not to be afraid (Mat 28:5). This was the angel recounted in Mark clothed in a long white robe sitting on the right side (Mark 16:5). The angel reassured them and told them not to be alarmed (Mark 16:6).
- The angels shifted positions, stood by the women (Luke 24:4-5), asked why they sought the living among the dead (Luke 24:5) and declared He was "not here, but is risen!" (Luke 24:6).
- The women then ran to tell Peter and John (John 20:2), who returned to inspect the tomb (John 20:3).
- The disciples returned to their homes (John 20:10), but Mary stood outside by the tomb

weeping and looked into the tomb (John 20:11), where she saw two angels in white sitting, one at the head and the other at the feet, where the body of Jesus had lain (John 20:12). They asked her why she was weeping (John 20:13). Mary then encountered Jesus (John 20:14).

3. Problem with Attempted Harmonization

The proposed explanation that the discrepancies between the accounts of the angels present at the tomb does not account for the fact that the various accounts contradict as to which angel said what:

- Matthew states that the angel who rolled back the stone and sat on it was the one who told the women not to be afraid, that Jesus was risen and to tell the disciples that He is going before them into Galilee. The angel said:
  o *"Do not be afraid, for I know that you seek Jesus who was crucified. He is not here; for He is risen, as He said. Come, see the place where the Lord lay. And go quickly and tell His disciples that He is risen from the dead, and indeed He is going before you into Galilee; there you will see Him. Behold, I have told you"* (Mat 28:5-7).

- Mark states that the young man sitting on the right side of the tomb (Mark 16:5) was the one who told the women not to be afraid, that Jesus was risen and to tell the disciples that He was going before them into Galilee. The angel said:
  o *"Do not be alarmed. You seek Jesus of Nazareth, who was crucified. He is risen! He is not here. See the place where they laid Him. But go, tell His disciples—and Peter—that He*

is going _before you into Galilee; there you will
see Him_, as He said to you" (Mark 16:6-7).

- Luke states that two men standing by the women
  in shining garments (Luke 24:4) said:
  o "_Why do you seek the living among the dead?
     He is not here, but is risen! Remember how He
     spoke to you when He was still in Galilee,
     saying, 'The Son of Man must be delivered into
     the hands of sinful men, and be crucified, and
     the third day rise again._" (Luke 24:5-7).

- John states that Mary Magdalene went to the
  tomb, found it empty and then told Peter and John,
  who went to inspect it. After Peter and John
  departed, Mary stood outside by the tomb
  weeping. Mary then saw two angels in white
  sitting, one at the head and the other at the feet,
  where the body of Jesus had lain (John 20:12).
  The angels said to her:
  o "_Woman, why are you weeping?_" (John 20:13)

There thus appears to be a discrepancy between who
said what. According to Matthew, it was the angel sitting
on the stone who told the women not to be afraid, that
Jesus was risen and to tell the disciples that He is going
before them into Galilee. According to Mark, it was the
angel inside the tomb who spoke these words. According
to Luke, both angels inside the tomb reported that Jesus
was not there and was risen.

4. Reply

It is possible that the angel who sat on the stone in
Matthew was the angel that was inside the tomb in Mark.
When the women first arrived, he sitting on the stone.
However, at the point where he tells the women not to be
afraid (Mat 28:5 and Mark 16:6), he had moved into the

tomb. We do not have a sense in Matthew as to how much time elapsed between when the women first encountered the angel sitting on the stone in Matthew 28:2 and when the angel spoke to them in Matthew 28:5. It appears that between his first appearance and the words he spoke to the women, the guards "shook for fear of him, and became like dead men" (Mat 28:4). It is possible that during this drama, the angel moved into the tomb and was thus the angel sitting on the right in the tomb reported in Mark 16:5. Matthew does not state that at the time the angel spoke to the women that he was still sitting on the stone. It is thus possible that the angel that was sitting on the stone was the same angel that spoke to Mary from within the tomb.

Luke gives an account of two angels sitting in the tomb. These angels could have been the first angel who rolled away the stone, entered the tomb and spoke to the women in Matthew 28:5 and Mark 16:6 and a second angel who accompanied him. Luke's account appears to be an abbreviation of Matthew's and Mark's account, where Luke, like Matthew and Mark, recounts that the angel said Jesus was "not here" and had "risen," but does not given the instruction to not be afraid, to tell the disciples and to meet Jesus in Galilee. Luke does not state that the words he recounted were the only words that the angels spoke. Therefore, this is not necessarily a contradiction. Moreover, it is possible that the angel that initially sat on the stone told the women that Jesus was "not here" and was "risen" and the second angel spoke the words about how Jesus "spoke to you when He was still in Galilee, saying, 'The Son of Man must be delivered into the hands of sinful men, and be crucified, and the third day rise again'" (Luke 24:7). Luke therefore recounts that "they" (the angels) spoke to the women, whereas Matthew and Mark recount only the words of the first angel.

In John, the angels are only reported to ask the question "Woman, why are you weeping?" (John 20:13). Matthew, Mark and Luke do not report this question. It is thus possible that the first or the second angel asked Mary this question before or after the first angel spoke the words reported in Matthew, Mark and Luke. Again, none of the Evangelists state that the words they reported were the "only" words spoken by the angel(s). Therefore, the words of the angels recounted in John do not amount to a contradiction.

VII.   THE WORDS OF THE ANGELS AND JESUS TO MARY

1. The Angels' Words

a. Overview

Matthew	Mark	Luke	John
Mat 28:5 But *the* *angel* answered and said to the women,	Mark 16:6 But *he* said to them,	Luke 24:5 Then, as they were afraid and bowed their faces to the earth, *they* said to them,	John 20:13 Then they said to her,
"Do not be afraid,	"Do not be alarmed.		
for I know that you seek Jesus who was crucified. Mat 28:6	You seek Jesus of Nazareth, who was crucified. He is risen! He	"Why do you seek the living among the dead? Luke 24:6 He is not	

He is <u>not</u> here; for He is <u>risen</u>,	is <u>not here</u>.	<u>here</u>, but is <u>risen</u>!	
as He said. Come, <u>see</u> <u>the place</u> <u>where the Lord lay</u>.	<u>See the place</u> where they laid Him.		
		Remember how He spoke to you when He was still in Galilee, Luke 24:7 saying, 'The Son of Man must be delivered into the hands of sinful men, and be crucified, and the third day rise again.' "	
Mat 28:7 And <u>go</u> quickly and <u>tell</u> <u>His</u> <u>disciples</u>	Mark 16:7 But <u>go</u>, <u>tell</u> <u>His</u> <u>disciples</u>— and Peter—		
that He is risen from	that <u>He is</u> <u>going before</u>		

the dead, and indeed He is going before you into Galilee; there you will see Him. Behold, I have told you."	you into Galilee; there you will see Him, as He said to you."		
			"Woman, why are you weeping?"

b. Explanation

The accounts of the words of the angels do not constitute contradictions:

- The accounts in Matthew and Mark are largely identical;
- The account in Luke appears to be a summary of the words spoken in Matthew and Mark; and
- The account in John appears to be a question spoken by the angels in addition to the words spoken in the other accounts, without contradicting them.

2. Jesus' Words

a. Overview

Matthew	**John**

Mat 28:9 And as they went to tell His disciples, behold, Jesus met them, saying, *"Rejoice!"* So they came and held Him by the feet and worshiped Him. Mat 28:10 Then Jesus said to them,	John 20:15 Jesus said to her,
	"Woman, why are you weeping? Whom are you seeking?" She, supposing Him to be the gardener, said to Him, "Sir, if You have carried Him away, tell me where You have laid Him, and I will take Him away." John 20:16 Jesus said to her, *"Mary!"* She turned and said to Him, "Rabboni!" (which is to say, Teacher). John 20:17 Jesus said to her, *"Do not cling to Me, for I have not yet ascended to My Father;*
"Do not be afraid.	
Go and tell My brethren	*but go to My brethren and say to them,*
to go to Galilee, and there they will see Me."	
	'I am ascending to My Father and your Father, and to My God and your God.' "

b. Explanation

Jesus could have spoken all of the words reported in Matthew and John to Mary. There is no contradiction in saying:

- "Rejoice! <u>Do not be afraid</u>. Go and <u>tell My brethren to go to Galilee</u>, and there they will see Me" (Mat 28:9-10); on the one hand, and
- "Woman, <u>why are you weeping</u>? <u>Whom are you seeking</u>? Mary! Do not cling to Me, for I have not yet ascended to My Father; but <u>go to My brethren and say to them, 'I am ascending to My Father and your Father, and to My God and your God.'"</u> (John 20:15-17), on the other hand.

c. Potential Issues

The potential issue in these accounts is there appears to be so much overlap between some of the words of the angels and those of Jesus that some of the Evangelists may have mistaken who said what, attributing the words of Jesus to the angels. Most notably:

- According to Matthew, Jesus says, "Do not be <u>afraid</u>. <u>Go and tell My brethren</u> to <u>go to Galilee</u>, and <u>there they will see Me</u>" (Mat 28:10).
- Mark, however, gives no account of Mary's encounter with Jesus and attributes almost the exact same words to the angel, who said, "Do not be <u>alarmed</u>. But <u>go</u>, <u>tell His disciples</u>—and Peter—that <u>He is going before you into Galilee</u>; <u>there you will see Him</u>, as He said to you" (Mark 16:6-7).

d. Explanation

It is possible that both Jesus and the angel spoke these words. Indeed, this is the account given by both Matthew and John, where Jesus' words echo and repeat the words of the angel spoken just verses earlier. Of note:

- Matthew attributes substantially similar words to both the angel and Jesus:
  o The angel says, "Do not be <u>afraid</u> … <u>go</u> quickly and <u>tell His disciples</u> … <u>He is going before you into Galilee</u>; <u>there you will see Him</u>"(Mat 28:5-7);
  o Jesus says, just a few verses later, "Do not be <u>afraid</u>. <u>Go and tell My brethren</u> to <u>go to Galilee</u>, and <u>there they will see Me</u>" (Mat 28:9).

We thus know that in His later encounter with Mary, Jesus repeated much of what the angel told Mary. This is fully within the realm of the possible. Both the angel and Jesus were sent by God and it is entirely plausible that they would both deliver similar messages to Mary, reinforcing the instructions to be given to the disciples.

- John attributes identical words to the angel and to Jesus:
  o In John 20:13, the angel asks, "<u>Woman, why are you weeping?</u>"
  o John gives an account of Jesus asking this very same question just two verses later in John 20:15, "<u>Woman, why are you weeping?</u>"

This is not a matter of two Evangelists misattributing the same words to two different individuals; rather, it is a case of the same Evangelists reporting that two individuals spoke the same words, which is entirely within the realm of the possible.

VIII. DID MARY MAGDALENE INFORM THE DISCIPLES OF THE EMPTY TOMB?

1. Apparent Contradiction 1: Mark States Mary Magdalene "Said Nothing to Anyone," But Matthew, Luke and John State that Mary Told the Disciples

a. Overview

a. Matthew: Yes, to the disciples

Mat 28:5 But the angel answered and said to the women, "Do not be afraid, for I know that you seek Jesus who was crucified.
Mat 28:6 He is not here; for He is risen, as He said. Come, see the place where the Lord lay.
Mat 28:7 And go quickly and <u>tell His disciples that He is risen from the dead, and indeed He is going before you into Galilee</u>; there you will see Him. Behold, I have told you."
Mat 28:8 So they went out quickly from the tomb with fear and great joy, and <u>ran to bring His disciples word</u>.
Mat 28:9 And as they went to tell His disciples, behold, Jesus met them, saying, "Rejoice!" So they came and held Him by the feet and worshiped Him.

b. Mark: No

Mark was a disciple of Peter. One would expect that he would have if Mary Magdalene had told Peter of the empty tomb, as reported in John 20:2, then Mark would have reported this. Instead, Mark states that Mary Magdalene "said nothing to anyone," for she was afraid:

> Mark 16:5 And entering the tomb, they saw a young man clothed in a long white robe sitting on the right side; and they were alarmed.
> Mark 16:6 But he said to them, "Do not be alarmed. You seek Jesus of Nazareth, who was crucified. He is risen! He is not here. See the place where they laid Him.
> Mark 16:7 But go, tell His disciples—and Peter—that He is going before you into Galilee; there you will see Him, as He said to you."
> Mark 16:8 So they went out quickly and fled from the tomb, for they trembled and were amazed. And they said nothing to anyone, for they were afraid.

c. *Luke: Yes, to the eleven and all the rest*

> Luke 24:3 Then they went in and did not find the body of the Lord Jesus.
> Luke 24:4 And it happened, as they were greatly perplexed about this, that behold, two men stood by them in shining garments.
> Luke 24:5 Then, as they were afraid and bowed their faces to the earth, they said to them, "Why do you seek the living among the dead?
> Luke 24:6 He is not here, but is risen! Remember how He spoke to you when He was still in Galilee,
> Luke 24:7 saying, 'The Son of Man must be delivered into the hands of sinful men, and be crucified, and the third day rise again.' "
> Luke 24:8 And they remembered His words.
> Luke 24:9 Then they returned from the tomb and told all these things to the eleven and to all the rest.

d. *John: Yes, but only to Peter and John*

> John 20:1 Now the first day of the week Mary Magdalene went to the tomb early, while it was still dark, and saw that the stone had been taken away from the tomb.
> John 20:2 Then she ran and came to Simon Peter, and to the other disciple, whom Jesus loved, and said to them, "They have taken away the Lord out of the tomb, and we do not know where they have laid Him."

b. Proposed Explanation: Mark Only Means that the Women
    Said Nothing to Anyone Immediately

By "said nothing to anyone," Mark may have meant that the
women said nothing to anyone immediately after they witnessed
the empty tomb and the angel. In their immediately fear, they
may have been awestruck and speechless, but they may have
eventually told Peter and John upon their encounter with them.

The use of the word "then" in the NKJV translation of the
Bible in John 20:2 does not necessarily mean that Mary
Magdalene immediately informed Peter and John. In fact, other
versions of the verse do not include this word, but instead use
"so" or "therefore," implying that the word "then" is not
intended to mean "immediately" but rather "therefore." For
example:

> (ASV) She runneth therefore, and cometh to Simon Peter, and
> to the other disciple whom Jesus loved, and saith unto them,
> They have taken away the Lord out of the tomb, and we know
> not where they have laid him.
> (Darby) She runs therefore and comes to Simon Peter, and to
> the other disciple, to whom Jesus was attached, and says to
> them, They have taken away the Lord out of the tomb, and
> we know not where they have laid him.
> (ESV) So she ran and went to Simon Peter and the other
> disciple, the one whom Jesus loved, and said to them, "They
> have taken the Lord out of the tomb, and we do not know
> where they have laid him."
> (ISV) So she ran off and went to Simon Peter and the other
> disciple, whom Jesus kept loving. She told them, "They have
> taken the Lord out of the tomb, and we don't know where
> they have put him!"
> (NIrV) So she ran to Simon Peter and another disciple, the
> one Jesus loved. She said, "They have taken the Lord out of
> the tomb! We don't know where they have put him!"
> (NIV) So she came running to Simon Peter and the other
> disciple, the one Jesus loved, and said, "They have taken the
> Lord out of the tomb, and we don't know where they have put
> him!"
> (RSV) So she ran, and went to Simon Peter and the other
> disciple, the one whom Jesus loved, and said to them, "They
> have taken the Lord out of the tomb, and we do not know
> where they have laid him."

Therefore, it is possible that Mary Magdalene, for fear, did not immediately tell anyone of the empty tomb and encounter with the angel, but then later told Peter and John, but Mark did not report this.

c. Proposed Explanation: Mary Magdalene Told Peter and John, but Mark Did not Report This

The account in Mark states, "they went out quickly and fled from the tomb, for they trembled and were amazed. And they said nothing to anyone, for they were afraid" (Mark 16:8). It is possible, however, that Mary did in fact tell Peter and John (or some other disciples) but Mark did not report it because he was either:

- unaware of this, as he was not present (recall Mark was not one of the 12 Apostles; he was a later disciple of Peter), and thus did not report it;
- aware of it, but in stating "they said nothing to anyone," he only meant initially and did not give the further detail of their account to Peter and John because he structured his account as a summary that did not include every details included in the other Gospel accounts. He may not have included this detail, particularly if he was trying to express the extent of Mary's awe, fear and wonder, which may have left her paralyzed and speechless, at least initially, until she encountered Peter, John and/or other disciples, at which point she very naturally would have recounted to them what she saw.

2. **Apparent Contradiction 2: Matthew States Mary Magdalene told "His Disciples"; Luke States She Told "the Eleven and All the Rest"; John States She Told Peter and John**

a. Overview

Matthew states Mary Magdalene told "His disciples"; Luke states she told "the eleven and to all the rest" and John states she told "Peter and John."

b. Proposed Explanation: Mary Magdalene Informed All the Disciples, but the Evangelists Give Varying Accounts Based on Their Focus

These differences are not necessarily contradictions. It is entirely possible that Mary did in fact tell the eleven disciples and to "all the rest," but that:

- Matthew does not give this additional detail; he merely states that she told "the disciples";
- Mark does not give this information, as he may have been unaware as he was not present or he was aware but opted to omit it as an unnecessary detail;
- John gives only part of the account, focusing on the portion that he witnessed, where Mary informed him and Peter, who then ran together to the tomb. It is entirely possible that either before or after Mary informed Peter and John, she informed the remaining disciples, or that the 11 disciples and others were together at the time that Mary informed Peter and John, but John opted to emphasize only his and Peter's encounter with Mary and their running to the tomb.

www.ingramcontent.com/pod-product-compliance
Lightning Source LLC
LaVergne TN
LVHW051253080426
835509LV00020B/2951